Crime Scene Processing
Laboratory Manual and Workbook

Crime Scene Processing Laboratory Manual and Workbook

Donald A. Hayden

CRC PRESS

Boca Raton   London   New York   Washington, D.C.

Library of Congress Cataloging-in-Publication Data

Hayden, Donald A.
  Crime scene processing laboratory manual / Donald A. Hayden.
       p.   cm.
  ISBN 0-8493-2103-4 (alk. paper)
1. Crime scene searches--Handbooks, manuals, etc. 2. Crime scene searches--Problems,
exercises, etc. 3. Crime laboratories--Handbooks, manuals, etc. 4. Crime laboratories--
Problems, exercises, etc. 5. Criminal investigation--Handbooks, manuals, etc. 6.
Evidence, Criminal--Handbooks, manuals, etc. I. Title.

HV8073.H32 2004
363.25--dc22
                                                                                    2004050300

Preface

When a crime is committed, evidence is normally present. This has been undisputed for many years. Sir Edmund Locard is indelibly linked to the fact that criminals will leave something at a crime scene and will take something with them. The job of the crime scene technician is to determine what is missing and what was left. Television continues to glamorize the job of the crime scene technician. The effects of television have made our job even more difficult. Offenders now know that they leave fingerprints, DNA material, or fiber evidence at a crime scene. Our challenge is to be even better at what we do. A true crime scene technician is not concerned with guilt or innocence but rather with gathering all of the facts possible at a crime scene and piecing the puzzle together to tell the story.

This crime scene processing laboratory manual is designed to teach the basics of crime scene documentation, evidence identification, evidence preservation, and evidence collection. You will conduct several hands-on practical exercises using different techniques. At the conclusion of each hands-on exercise, you will prepare a report of your findings and based upon those findings, make a determination as to which method works the best *for you*. As you will see, in many instances, there may be more than one correct method of accomplishing a task. A large part of the purpose of this manual is to provide you with simulated exercises prior to engaging in a real crime scene that you have to process.

You must understand that each of these exercises is only a slice of the pie that makes up crime scene processing. Crime scene documentation through complete and accurate notes, sketches, and photographs is oftentimes as important as the development of a fingerprint. There are myriad experts on both sides of a courtroom, and at least part of the job of the crime scene technician is to enable reconstruction of the scene. This can be accomplished only through proper documentation. To that end, a number of documentary exercises are included, either describing the scene portrayed in a photograph, drawing a sketch from notes provided, or photographing a hypothetical crime scene.

This manual has several specific objectives. They are:

- Provide hands-on learning in the rapidly evolving world of crime scene processing
- Learn what evidence is
- Successfully document a crime scene via notes, sketches, and photographs
- Identify evidence and proper collection methods
- Develop and collect items of evidence at a crime scene

Whether you are a first-year college student or an experienced investigator, the skills you will learn from this manual can never be underrated. You, the student, must understand that crime scene processing is neither glamorous nor completed in a 60-minute block of time. Perfectly accomplished but often mundane tasks are what set a true crime scene technician apart from the rest of the world. When you complete the exercises in this manual, not only will you have a far better ability to properly document and process a crime scene, but, because of the design of this manual, you will have a permanent reference you can use throughout your career.

It is important to note that this workbook is not a substitute for classroom lecture. This product is designed to enhance the information provided in lecture. I encourage you to mount your work in the spaces provided and keep this manual as a permanent record of your training and experience. This manual will serve as a great reference, and you may find that you will one day be the teacher — to prosecutors, juries, or even your fellow law enforcement officers.

About the Author

Mr. Hayden is a retired U.S. Army Criminal Investigations Command Special Agent. He served over 20 years in the U.S. Army, retiring in 2003. Among his varied assignments, Mr. Hayden was the chief of the Criminalistics and Crime Scenes Branch of the United States Army Military Police School for nearly 5 years. The experience garnered from that assignment and from nearly 18 years as a CID Special Agent forms the basis of knowledge from which this product emerged.

Mr. Hayden is currently an adjunct professor of Criminal Justice and Forensic Science at Columbia College, Columbia, Missouri, where he teaches the full spectrum of crime scenes-related courses.

Acknowledgments

Although this manual is a stand-alone document that can be used by students of criminal justice, forensic science, police academies, or other law enforcement training entities, I cannot thank Mr. Ross Gardner, the author of a new criminal investigation publication by CRC Press, enough for his knowledge, wisdom, and input into this workbook.

This workbook would not have been possible without the assistance of two true superstars in the world of crime scene processing, Mr. William D. Anderson and Mr. T. Geoff Lewis. Bill and Geoff, who are among my closest friends, provided the voice of reason concerning the exercises presented in this manual. They assisted me in assuring that the exercises in this manual were on target for the intended audience. Their reviews of drafts of this workbook proved invaluable.

General Instructions

This workbook has been prepared with perforated pages and with three prepunched holes. This will enable you to remove your completed exercises from the workbook and place them in a three-ring binder. If you make the full use of this workbook you should also take photographs which you attach to the provided pages as well as attach your fingerprint lifts, which will leave you a permanent record of your work and serve as a future reference.

It is important to note that none of these exercises is designed as a complete crime scene processing exercise. You must remember that at a real crime scene you will always document your crime scene activities via notes, sketches, and photographs prior to any actual hands-on destructive processing.

When you process a crime scene, you will no doubt process that scene as your training taught you. For that reason, you should always don rubber gloves (or Nitril if you have a latex intolerance).

Many of these exercises, if conducted at an actual crime scene, require that you wear personal protective equipment. Your instructor will no doubt, as part of his lecture, discuss personal protective measures. Take those lectures to heart. Many of the diseases you will encounter do not give you a second chance. Wear personal protective equipment during these exercises, and it will be second nature for you at a real crime scene.

Finally, although cleanup is not normally specifically documented, the prompt cleanup of your work area and equipment is vital to success. You should consider cleanup time and effort in your assessment.

Good luck in your exercises!

Table of Contents

Part **1**

Crime Scene Documentation

In this section you will expand your knowledge of those actions taken before you actually lay hands upon a crime scene. As you will see, the initial actions of a crime scene investigator set the stage for all subsequent actions.

The exercises in this section consist of word searches, prioritization exercises, and diagramming exercises.

You've been provided with plenty of space to document your observations. Take your time and remember, there is usually more than one solution to solving that puzzle known as crime scene documentation.

Exercise 1.1 Biological Hazard Protection

```
                    E
                  V J X
                A G M U F
              G R S C X A S
            L V N T Z C T T I
          S F M Q J V D D B N I
        T F D I P S P A U T E G C
      S V V Z H O J K C T W G F L K
    O O U A N P P A P Z Z S O R U P V
  R G M F R O J G L Q E R Z H P X O H X
E O N R Z G I E U G I I M N T Z M O B X J
D G Z V N O I T C E T O R P L A S R E V I N U
A D H D T T F T A G C R Y X T P P H R K N C D H G
H U M A N I M M U N O D E F I C I E N C Y V I R U S S
  D I N U F B W K I B C G E J B P N G E W W D O N V
    J D F Y Z L U M A Y U D Q A O R F T V P F Y F
      F Q C L T O A Q M L A T T H O I I Q P E Z
        W T T Q L T T D A I K A I B A X E S T
          O P Y Q N O U T U S A D D I N J O
            Q R L O K I E V T Z F O J Z E
              V M C S H D N H C V O D H
                P E O V W P G O K L C
                  D E S A G L J N B
                    H I S S S G R
                      M T Z D S
                        E N I
                          E
```

1. Any virus that is characterized by transmission via direct contact with contaminated blood
2. The process of cleaning persons and equipment after exposure to contaminated blood
3. A disease of the liver, often passed through direct contact with, for example, bloody needles
4. The virus that is the precursor to AIDS
5. An alternative type of glove worn by those individuals allergic to latex
6. Trash or other by-products produced at a crime scene that are potentially contaminated
7. Protective gear all crime scene personnel should wear.

Exercise 1.2 Crime Scene Prioritization

```
                M F
              N A N H
            E N E I D D
          G Z P X A S X O
        F G E F K R A V H V
      A M P I V Z J T W F O N
    T K H R Q K H I T V F Z O B
  Y J Q U O F Z Y L F H U N E N S
H N Q J F T G S E R P U G N C P C E
D I C A C I E L C U N O B I R Y X O E D
X K M K L E N C L A S S K E T C H Z G K Y P
K K U Z G F F G T S I U W V T I S G R T Y Q M O
F T U K R U W Q E I F S H D I P V H O R B P S W R N
P E R S O N A L P R O T E C T I V E E Q U I P M E N T I
J H P A R G O T O H P N E R S I B V L M C C L E L R Z N E S
B H A F I H F S K N R U I W M B H F I M L S Z K Z G N X A U
J P P B A N A V K J I S A J A C T K G D I D L Q O J O D O G
L G L N H M Z S F O N A E V M Q H R A X N L X P G T C S N A
R E L F D M X D J H T G V A G U T A R H I I R K M I F W E P
K W P G S Y E V X V M Q Y B I W L X F N L F P P Y Q Z D E I
```

1. A generalization of evidence that identifies an item to a similar group of like items
2. Individual characteristic evidence obtained from, for example, white blood cells
3. An example of fragile evidence, unique to each person, even identical twins
4. Evidence that will be easily destroyed if care is not taken
5. Evidence that, if not protected and expeditiously collected, will disappear and once gone, is gone forever
6. Evidence that could easily be replaced with similar items without notice
7. An example of trace evidence that can be shed, pulled, or cut, and that is difficult to protect
8. A generalization of evidence that identifies an item to the exclusion of all others
9. Protective gloves, goggles, masks, and foot covers
10. One of the noninvasive documentary methods, done before any other activity
11. Those measures you take at a crime scene to ensure evidence is not destroyed
12. Documenting a crime scene, also known as mapping

Exercise 1.3 Crime Scene Sketching

```
                  E L G
               H X G L L P K
             R V P S C J A H T K C
           G M L O V K J G C I Y D J
         E Y O Y L F L Q L R S T R L V
       F D C R A J C P J O I R A F P
     F E M H L R U C G A S F I L G D D
     D N O I T C E R I D S S A P M O C
   V S I A U V O N L J D P T N H T B S L
   G F L G E I O U K X M R I G A S V K G
   B C E E J F R P Q M H O I U N E K Q B
     G S K G F D Z C A H J H L U V U D
     D A C X E I P S R O E N A M S N O
       B N A C N Z F O U C S T E G Y
       I F X P A D F Y N T H I R J V
         O Q T T O D R Z I S O I P
           C W E I J D C O E N C
             S Z O Z Q N I
               N N D
```

1. The manner of differentiating between items of evidence and other items in the legend
2. The use of 90° measurements to document evidence positions from an imaginary line inserted into the crime scene
3. The heading of a crime scene diagram
4. That portion of a crime scene diagram that indicates which way is north
5. Also known as an exploded view; vertical surfaces are "laid down"
6. A diagram where all four walls, the ceiling, and the floor are attached and placed on one piece of paper; useful in blood spatter documentation
7. An overhead view of a crime scene
8. That area of a crime scene diagram where items of evidence and other items are identified
9. The documentation of evidence at a crime scene using magnetic compass directions from a known point in the crime scene
10. The indicator on a crime scene diagram of proportional distances
11. The fixing of items of evidence with measurements, also known as the two "v" method

Exercise 1.4 Evidence

```
J T M D Y Q J T R B Z D N A I X D F V H
E E W G A C Q B T F E P D S N E L L V P
D N Q L D D P H L P N B T L F A P C U F
Y F Z C N T H Z O U S E J D B C H O P E
W O N D F I W C Y D S R E O C A Y P J V
N B U T D Z O Q T T F X R I I S S D R E
V N U Q C J U D I C I A L N O T I C E H
D L N K Z E O M N F T O O O Q R C H P R
F H N F V D O W L O Q F C I I P A C D J
O A Z I K N S W R U C T B S K D L U N U
Q S A B I G T Y C U G H V S Z A E U Y U
C H B A Q C R J S U I X A E U X V C W T
T F L A T E N T F I N G E R P R I N T P
I T Y G P Z O P P D M V Y P T X D L R L
A T K O C D H Y Q K F C R M L A E C D R
H X R N Y M K O E U X R W I F L N L E U
U T D L K Z V F Z V Z L U J E P C I K G
W T F Y Q I I A B M O V E A B L E K R I
A L V Y Q I V S E G Z F M Y P U F W L D
H J T Z X F L E K Y L S H S C P Y X V B
```

1. The finished product when you pour dental stone into an impression
2. The document created to identify each individual who came into contact with a piece of evidence
3. Evidence prepared for demonstration in court
4. Anything that is part of an investiation that helps determine the truth
5. Evidence at a crime scene that cannot be moved
6. A latent or patent mark in soil that is three dimensional
7. Evidence that courts take as the truth, such as the day of the week
8. A document prepared by a forensic scientist to detail actions taken with evidence
9. An impression made by the hand that is not visible to the naked eye
10. Evidence that can be easily carried away from a crime scene
11. Evidence you can touch
12. Evidence that is the spoken or written word

Practical Exercise 1.5: Crime Scene Prioritization

The purpose of this section is to use logic and reasoning to determine what items at a crime scene are of significance. This exercise will also enable you to prioritize your activities at a crime scene. Finally, you will determine what actions you must take at a crime scene and in what order you will complete various actions.

Equipment Needed

1. Paper and pencil

Complete the Exercise

Read the following scenario and determine what, if anything, is evidence. In addition, determine what steps you need to take to preserve the evidence. Ensure you include an assessment of weather conditions, destructiveness of the collection process, location of the item, and so forth. Remember that the order in which you process a crime scene is imperative. Do first things first. In assessing the scene, explain what actions you would take to protect those items you determine to be evidence and the order and manner in which you would collect them. Do not forget that you will need to protect yourself as well. Last, explain your reasoning. Reasoning is the "why" of prioritization that ties all of your actions together. Remember, in crime scene processing, the order is not as important as the logic and reasoning you employ to make your decision. More than one correct solution set may exist for this exercise. Document your findings on the chart at the end of the scenario. You should have plenty of room to document your reasoning.

The Scenario

At 1930, March 17, you are notified of a death at 5310 East Hightower Street, Anytown, USA. You respond to the scene and upon arrival make the following observations.

> The weather conditions are as follows: it is 56° Fahrenheit, winds are from the north at 8 mph and heavy rain is predicted.

The scene is a three-story apartment complex and consists of 12 different apartments. The deceased person is located in apartment 3C. Apartment 3C is located on the third floor. Entry to the apartment can be gained by walking up the exterior stairwells. There are four apartment entryways on each landing. Entry to the landings on the second and third floors can also be made by riding an elevator that opens at the rear landing of the second and third floors. The landings are covered but are not enclosed.

As you approach the scene, you notice a green two-door GEO Storm in the parking space marked 3C. The vehicle is locked and does not appear to have been tampered with. There are no other nonemergency vehicles in the parking lot. (You are told that the reporting officers had the other vehicles removed from the parking lot.)

As you walk toward the stairwell, you notice there is a series of red stains in the shape of shoe impressions on the sidewalk. These shoe impressions appear to contain class characteristics, and you suspect they are composed of blood. There are four shoe prints present, all seem to be from the right foot and appear to have been made from the same shoe. The impressions lead from the elevator entry and disappear into the grass. You see a large knife in the bushes just to the right of the sidewalk near the base of the exterior wall of the apartment complex.

As you climb the stairwell to the third floor, you do not notice any further impressions. Upon arrival on the third floor landing, you see two footwear impressions (similar to those on the ground floor sidewalk) that lead toward the elevator entry on the third floor landing. There is a bloody fingerprint impression on the elevator call button. When you examine the interior of the elevator, you see another bloody shoe print on the floor and a bloody smear on the elevator ground floor button.

A uniformed patrol officer stands guard on the third floor landing. As you approach apartment 3C, you notice that the door is open; however, it does not appear to have been forced open.

Inside the small 1-bedroom apartment, the living room is in a state of disarray. (At this point, assume you will use a circle search pattern and proceed around the room in a counterclockwise direction.)

As you stand in the doorway, which is located along the south wall, to the left (west) is a galley-style kitchen which is about 5 ft deep and 6 ft wide, with a refrigerator, stove, and microwave. Counters surround three walls of the kitchen, with the refrigerator along the south wall, a double sink along the west wall of the kitchen, and the stove with the microwave mounted above it along the north wall of the kitchen. There is what looks to be standard kitchen equipment present randomly placed on the counters. Items present include a coffeemaker, a toaster, a set of canisters, a dish strainer with no dishes in it, and a wooden knife block. The block should contain nine knives, however, only eight are present. The space in the block for what appears to be the largest knife is empty. The kitchen floor is light beige vinyl sheeting.

To the right (east) of the doorway along the south wall is a large living/dining room. The living room is about 15 ft by 15 ft. Directly adjacent to the doorway on the east side is a brown leather recliner. The recliner sits at an angle along the south wall facing to the north and west. On the east side of the recliner is a brass color floor lamp. Next to the lamp is a brown wooden end table with a candy dish on it.

Heavy green drapes from floor to ceiling cover the entire east wall. The drapes are pulled closed. A large, perhaps 25 in., console television is in the approximate center of the east wall directly under the picture window and about 6 in. from the east wall. A Philips brand clock radio sits in the approximate center of the top of the television. In the southeast corner of the room on the floor is a gold color frame with broken glass. The frame holds an 8 × 10 in. photograph of a woman (apparently the deceased). The glass is broken and both the frame and the glass shards that remain in the frame are bloodied and appear to have bloody fingerprints on them. On the back of the photograph, handwritten script reads "Jim and Caroline in Cabo."

Along the north wall of the living room is a brown leather couch, made of material similar to the recliner. On both ends of the couch are brown wooden end tables, each with a table lamp atop it. The deceased woman lies on the couch. The woman, who appears to be a slender blonde-haired Caucasian in her mid-20s, is clothed in a pair of gray sweat shorts and a crop-top gray sweatshirt. Her hair is in a pony tail and appears to be shoulder length. She is wearing a minor amount of facial makeup. There are no apparent injuries to the facial area. The woman is barefoot. Visible on the woman's chest, just below the bottom edge of the crop-top sweatshirt, are three apparent stab wounds.

A large amount of blood is on the woman's chest, and blood has pooled on the couch cushions. An examination of the woman's hands reveals that her right hand is clenched and appears to be holding a piece of white cloth. From the rough size of the material it appears that it could be the pocket from a white dress shirt.

About 1 ft, 6 in. in front of and centered directly in front of the couch is a glass top coffee table, about 4-ft long. Two clear glass "rocks" glasses are on the table. Both glasses are partially full and contain an amber liquid. The liquid smells like beer. On the coffee table is a piece of paper, which appears to be an unfolded letter. The writing on the letter states in part: "Dearest Jim, Although you will always be my first love. . . . I have found someone else who understands my needs. . . . Always, Caroline."

Several bloody footprints (similar to those found outside) lead from the couch to the front door and out to the elevator.

A cursory review of the remainder of the apartment, which consists of a bedroom and a full bathroom, reveals no other items of interest.

Document Your Observations

In the space provided below, document what you identify as evidence and the order in which you would collect it, the manner of preservation, and your logic:

Item to Be Preserved	Preservation Measures	Reasoning

Crime Scene Prioritization Notes

To complete this exercise, you need to document your findings. Include factors such as why you chose the order you chose; what additional information you would need to gather; what fragile, fugitive, or fungible evidence is present. What about crime scene security?

NOTES

Practical Exercise 1.6: Basic and Projection Sketching

The purpose of this section is to prepare an overview of a written crime scene via sketches or crime scene diagrams. In this exercise, a very basic room with items of furniture and only minimal evidence has been included. You will draw a total of five sketches or diagrams for this exercise. Ensure that you label your sketch with all of the key elements of a sketch and identify pieces of furniture separately from pieces of evidence.

Equipment Needed

1. Pencil
2. Paper
3. Ruler

Complete the Exercise

Read the following scenario. Extract the key points and prepare a crime scene sketch on the accompanying sheets of paper.

The Scenario

At 0600, January 2, you are dispatched to a residential burglary complaint at 12573 East Locust Street, Union City. You arrive at about 0630 and discover a red brick two-story house that had been broken into via the rear bedroom window. It was reported that at about 0530, January 2, Mr. Fred Smith returned home from work and discovered his bedroom window open. Upon investigating, he discovered the glass in the window had been broken and his portable color television was missing from his bedroom. Your assessment of the scene reveals that entry was gained via breaking the bedroom window. When you examine the room this is what you find:

The Room

(Assume that you will use a circle search pattern, beginning at the north wall and traversing clockwise around the room.) The room contains four walls, each extending from the floor to the ceiling and each made out of standard drywall, painted white. The ceiling is level and 8 ft off the floor. The flooring consists of beige woven carpet which is in good condition. A surface-mounted ceiling light is in the approximate center of the ceiling. The fixture is 12 by 12 in., is covered by an opaque glass square, and has two light bulbs in it, both of which are on.

The North Wall

The north wall (which is the wall with the window that was broken) is 14 ft from east to west. The window is a 3-ft wide by 4-ft high double-sash window, 3 ft off the floor and 4 ft from the east wall. There is a hole in the lower half of the window. The hole is 8 in. wide and 6 in. high. The bottom window sash is halfway open. The size of the opening is 1 ft, 2 in. No screen is in the window. Directly below the window is an overstuffed easy chair. The chair is made of brown leather material. The chair sits flush against the wall and is centered below the window. The chair measures 2 ft, 6 in. from east to west, 2 ft, 8 in. from south to north and 3 ft high at the top of the backrest. The seat portion is 1 ft, 6 in. tall. On the headrest portion of the chair and on the seat area are a number of pieces of broken glass. The glass is consistent in appearance with the window above the chair. Next to the chair (to the east) is a four-drawer chest of drawers. The back of the chest of drawers is flush against the north wall and is 4 ft from the northeast corner of the room. The chest of drawers is 3 ft wide, 3 ft, 6 in. tall, and 1 ft, 6 in. deep. The chest is made of wood material and is a natural oak color. The four drawers are of equal size, each 8 in. tall. Four framed pictures of a woman are randomly arranged on the east side of the top of the chest of drawers.

The East Wall

The east wall is 12 ft long from north to south. There are no windows in the east wall. A large (2 ft wide by 3 ft high) painting of a vase with flowers is in the approximate center of the wall. The northern edge of the painting is 3 ft, 8 in. from the northeast corner of the room. The bottom of the painting is 3 ft, 8 in. off the floor and the painting is level. Directly below the painting is a six-drawer dresser. The north edge of the dresser is 2 ft from the northeast corner of the room. The dresser is 5 ft long, 2 ft, 8 in. high and 1 ft, 8 in. deep. The dresser is composed of wood material in a natural oak color. The six drawers are arranged in two equal columns of three drawers and each drawer is 8 in. high. A number of personal hygiene items (deodorant, cologne, a hair brush, and a pair of nail clippers) are on the top of the dresser. These items are all randomly placed on the northern half of the dresser top. A small statue of a horse is also on the dresser. The horse is roughly centered on the dresser. In the southeast corner of the room, on an angle, is a wicker clothes hamper. The hamper is 1 ft, 6 in. wide, 10 in. deep, and 2 ft, 8 in. high. The hamper is generally centered in the corner and about 2 in. away from both the east and south walls at their closest points.

The South Wall

The south wall is 14 ft long from east to west. The bed is 3 ft from the southeast corner of the room. The bed is a standard queen size "sleigh" bed made of natural oak color wood. The sleigh bed is 6 ft, 6 in. long, and 5 ft wide. The headboard of the bed is 3 ft, 10 in. tall and solid wood in appearance. The headboard is generally parallel to the south wall, about 2 in. away from the wall. The top of the mattress is 2 ft, 8 in. off the ground. The bed is made. The top blanket is a solid brown quilt and there are two pillows. The bed has a white fitted sheet and a white flat sheet, and both pillows are contained in white pillow cases. In the approximate center of the bed is a red brick. The brick is of construction similar to those from the exterior of the house. The brick is 4 in. wide, 8 in. long, and 2 in. thick. On the west side of the bed, about 4 in. from the west edge of the mattress is a nightstand. The nightstand is 1 ft, 6 in. wide, 1 ft, 10 in. deep, and 2 ft high. The front of the nightstand contains a drawer that is 4 in. high and flush with the underside of the table top. A wooden shelf is on the bottom of the nightstand. The square wooden legs are 2 in. thick. The nightstand is made of the same natural oak color wood as the rest of the furniture in the room. Sitting atop the nightstand and roughly centered is a table lamp. The table lamp is made of ceramic material in a "vase" configuration. The lamp has a linen shade that is off-white color. The lamp shade is 10 in. in diameter and is a cylinder. The lamp is 1 ft, 6 in. high. A 60-watt lightbulb is in the fixture and the light is on. The cord to the lamp trails behind the nightstand and plugs into a standard two socket electric outlet behind the table. The bottom of the outlet is 1 ft, 6 in. off the floor. Sitting in front of the lamp on the nightstand is a General Electric brand, model 3332x clock radio. The radio appears to be working and has the correct time. The electric cord for the clock radio trails behind the table and plugs into the same electric outlet as the lamp. Also atop the nightstand is a GE television remote. Next to the remote is a *TV Guide* for the current week. Continuing west along the south wall, next to the nightstand is the door. The door frame is a white painted wood construction. The door frame has a 3-in.-wide molding on both sides and on the top. The door entryway dimensions are 3 ft, 2-in. wide by 6 ft, 6-in. high. The door is a six-panel white wooden door that opens inward. The door knob is a brass Kwikset brand knob and appears in working order. The standard brass color hinges are on the western edge of the door. The doorknob has a push-button lock. The west edge of the door is 10 in from the southwest wall. There are no pictures on the south wall.

The West Wall

The west wall is 12 ft long from south to north and contains the closet. The closet is 12 in. north of the southwest corner of the room. The closet is 6 ft wide. A 3-in.-wide wooden molding surrounds the sides and tops of the closet doors. The top of the molding on the top of the closet is 6 ft, 9 in. off the ground and is level. The closet consists of two full-length mirrored sliding doors. Each door is 3 ft, 2 in. wide and they overlap by 2 in. The contents of the closet are not described here. In the northwest corner of the room is a wooden table that appears to be a television stand. The stand is 2 ft, 8 in. tall, 2 ft, 6 in. wide, and 1 ft, 8 in. deep. The stand is made of the same natural oak color wood. The stand sits on an angle in the corner 2 in. from the north and west walls and generally equally situated. The stand has two wooden shelves. The bottom is 8 in. off the ground. A stack of magazines lies on the shelf. The upper shelf is 1 ft, 10 in. off the floor and contains a wooden jewelry box which is 8 in. wide, 4 in. tall, and 6 in. deep. The box is nondecorative and appears to have been handmade. On the top of the television stand a void area in the dust indicates something had been present. The void area is 1 ft, 3 in. wide and 1 ft, 2 in. deep.

Document Your Activity

To complete this exercise, you will prepare five sketches. Include all of the key elements in the sketch. Include appropriate measurements and document all items of furniture and evidence on the accompanying sheets. First, draw a flat or bird's-eye-view sketch, then draw a flat or cross-projection sketch of each of the four walls.

Exercise 1.6   Crime Scene Sketch: Birdseye or Flat

Exercise 1.6 (continued)   **Crime Scene Sketch: Exploded View**

Exercise 1.6 (continued)   **Crime Scene Sketch: Exploded View**

Exercise 1.6 (continued)   **Crime Scene Sketch: Exploded View**

Exercise 1.6 (continued)   **Crime Scene Sketch: Exploded View**

NOTES

Practical Exercise 1.7: Triangulation Measurement

The purpose of this section is to document measurements obtained at a crime scene through sketches or crime scene diagrams. In this exercise, you will use the two-V method of measurement. In the two-V method of measurement, you measure to a specific point on opposite sides of a solid object such as a weapon, while you measure to the center of mass on irregularly shaped objects such as footprints or bloodstains. In this exercise, a very basic bedroom, with items of furniture and several items of evidence, has been described. Your challenge is to document those measurements in a crime scene sketch. Ensure that you include all of the key elements of a sketch and identify pieces of furniture separately from pieces of evidence.

Equipment Needed

1. Pencil
2. Paper
3. Ruler

Complete the Exercise

The following measurements are provided for you to complete the sketch:

Physical Aspects of the Room

The Walls

The north and south walls are 16 ft from west to east.

The east and west walls are 13 ft from south to north.

There is a 3-in. tall, 1/2-in. thick molding surrounding the entire base of the wall at the floor.

The Doors

The main entry/exit door is in the east wall. The door is 3 ft wide and the southernmost edge, which is the side with the hinges, is 6 in. from the southeast corner of the room.

A 3-ft-wide closet door on the south wall opens into the room. The easternmost edge of the door, which contains the hinges, is 2 ft, 6 in. from the southeast corner of the room. This door leads to a walk-in closet (which is outside the scope of this sketch).

The Windows

Window number one: there is a 3-ft long and 3-ft high window in the west wall.

Using a plumb bob to obtain a point directly below the southern edge of the window, the window is 6 ft from the southwest corner of the room and is level.

The bottom edge of the 2-in. thick window sill is 3 ft, 2 in. off the floor and is level.

Window number two: there is a 6-ft long, 3-ft high window in the south wall.

Using a plumb bob to obtain a point directly below the western edge of the window, the window is 4 ft from the southwest corner of the room.

The bottom edge of the 2-in. thick window sill is 3 ft, 2 in. off the floor and is level.

The Furniture

Nightstand number one

There is a nightstand in the northwest corner of the room.

The nightstand is 2 ft wide, 2 ft deep, and 2 ft, 6 in. high.

The back of the nightstand is flush against the north wall.

The western edge of the nightstand is 6 in. from the west wall.

The bed

There is a queen-size bed on the north wall.

The bed is 5 ft, 6 in. wide and 6 ft, 6 in. long.

The back of the headboard is flush against the north wall.

The western edge of the bed is 6 in. east of the easternmost point of nightstand number one.

Nightstand number two

On the east side of the bed is a nightstand which is identical to the one described previously.

The nightstand is 2 ft wide, 2 ft deep, and 2 ft, 6 in. high.

The back of the nightstand is flush against the north wall.

The western edge of the nightstand is 6 in. from the eastern edge of the bed.

The chest of drawers

There is a four-drawer chest of drawers along the north wall.

The chest of drawers is 3 ft wide, 1 ft, 8 in. deep, and 3 ft, 8 in. tall.

The back of the chest of drawers is flush against the north wall.

The eastern edge of the chest of drawers is 6 in. from the east wall.

The dresser

There is a six-drawer (two columns of three drawers) dresser on the east wall.

The dresser is 4 ft wide, 1 ft, 8 in. deep, and 3 ft, 8 in. tall.

The back of the dresser is flush against the east wall.

The northeast corner of the dresser is 4 ft, 6 in. from the northeast corner of the room.

The television stand

There is a television stand in the southwest corner of the room.

The television stand is 2 ft, 6 in. wide, 2 ft deep, and 2 ft, 8 in. high.

The back of the television stand is flush against the south wall.

The western edge of the television stand is 6 in. from the west wall of the room.

There is an area of dust on top of the television stand that is 2 ft, 3 in. wide and 1 ft, 2 in. deep. The area of dust is at an angle that would indicate that a television on the stand recently was canted toward the bed.

The Evidence

The Pistol

There is a Colt 45 semiautomatic pistol on its left side with the barrel facing the chest of drawers.

The leading edge of the front sight is 1 ft, 4 in. from the southeast corner of nightstand number two.

The leading edge of the front sight is 1 ft, 8 in. from the southwest corner of the chest of drawers.

The southernmost point of the magazine well is 2 ft, 8 in. from the northwest corner of the dresser.

The southernmost point of the magazine well is 5 ft, 6 in. from the southwest corner of the dresser.

Footprint Number One

There is an apparent bloody shoeprint on the floor. The toe portion of the shoeprint points roughly from the bed to the entryway.

The center of the shoeprint is 4 ft, 6 in. from the southwest corner of nightstand number two.

The center of the shoeprint is 2 ft, 8 in. from the southeast corner of the bed.

Footprint Number Two

There is a second apparent bloody shoeprint on the floor. This shoeprint also points in the direction of the entryway.

The center of the shoeprint is 1 ft, 6 in. from the southwest corner of the dresser.

The center of the shoeprint is 3 ft from the northern edge of the doorway.

The Shell Casing

There is a shell casing on the floor near the foot of the bed.

The primer end of the shell casing is 5 ft, 3 in. from the southeast corner of the television stand.

The primer end of the shell casing is 6 ft, 6 in. from the western edge of the closet doorway.

The open end of the shell casing is 2 ft, 6 in. from the southwest corner of the bed.

The open end of the shell casing is 3 ft, 8 in. southeast corner of the bed.

The Body

Note that all blankets and sheets had been removed prior to crime scene examination.

The head

The apex of the head is 3 ft, 10 in. from the northwest corner of the mattress.
The apex of the head is 1 ft, 10 in. from the northeast corner of the mattress.

The left hand

The little finger on the left hand is 3 ft, 4 in. from the northeast corner of the mattress.
The little finger on the left hand is 3 ft, 8 in. from the southeast corner of the mattress.

The legs
    The legs are both straight out. The left heel is 3 in. across. There is a space of 8 in. between the left and right foot.

The left foot
    The heel of the left foot is 4 ft, 4 in. from the southwest corner of the mattress.
    The heel of the left foot is 2 ft, 1 in. from the southeast corner of the mattress.

The right foot
    The heel of the right foot is 6 ft, 2 in. from the northwest corner of the mattress.
    The heel of the right foot is 3 ft, 6 in. from the southwest corner of the mattress.

The right arm is on top of the body therefore no measurement could be made.

Document Your Activity

To complete this exercise, prepare a two-V measurement sketch on the page provided. Note that you will be able to document only the items described. Include all of the key elements of the sketch. Include appropriate measurements and document all items of furniture and evidence.

Exercise 1.7   Evidence Measurement Sketch: Two-V Method

NOTES

Practical Exercise 1.8: Baseline Measurement

The purpose of this exercise is to document measurements obtained at a crime scene through sketches or crime scene diagrams. In this exercise, you will use the "baseline method" of measurements. In baseline measurement, you measure to the center of mass of your objects. In this exercise, a very basic bedroom, with items of furniture and several items of evidence, has been described. Your challenge is to document those measurements in your crime scene sketch. Ensure that you include all of the key elements of a sketch and identify pieces of furniture separately from pieces of evidence.

Equipment Needed

1. Pencil
2. Paper
3. Ruler

Complete the Exercise

The following measurements are provided for you to complete the sketch:

Physical Aspects of the Room

The Walls

The north and south walls are 16 ft from west to east.

The east and west walls are 13 ft from south to north.

There is a 3-in. tall, 1/2-in. thick molding surrounding the entire base of the wall at the floor.

The Doors

The main entry/exit door is in the east wall. The door is 3 ft wide and the southernmost edge, which is the side with the hinges and which opens inward, is 6 in. from the southeast corner of the room.

A 3-ft wide closet door on the south wall opens into the room. The easternmost edge of the door, which contains the hinges, is 2 ft, 6 in. from the southeast corner of the room. This door leads to a walk-in closet (which is outside the scope of this sketch).

The Windows

Window number one: there is a 3-ft long and 3-ft high window in the west wall.

Using a plumb bob to determine a point on the floor directly below the southern edge of the window, the window is 6 ft from the southwest corner of the room and is level.

The bottom edge of the 2-in. thick windowsill is 3 ft, 2 in. off the floor and is level.

Window number two: there is a 6-ft long, 3-ft high window in the south wall.

Using a plumb bob to determine a point on the floor directly below the western edge of the window, the window is 4 ft from the southwest corner of the room.

The bottom edge of the 2 in. thick windowsill is 3 ft, 2 in. off the floor and is level.

The Furniture

Nightstand number one

There is a nightstand in the northwest corner of the room.

The nightstand is 2 ft wide, 2 ft deep, and 2 ft, 6-in. high.

The back of the nightstand is flush against the north wall.

The western edge of the nightstand is 6 in. from the west wall.

The bed

There is a queen-size bed on the north wall.

The bed is 5 ft, 6 in. wide and 6 ft, 6 in. long.

The back of the headboard is flush against the north wall.

The western edge of the bed is 6 in. east of the easternmost point of the first nightstand.

Nightstand number two

On the east side of the bed is a nightstand which is identical to the one previously described.

The nightstand is 2 ft wide, 2 ft deep, and 2 ft, 6 in. high.

The back of the nightstand is flush against the north wall.

The western edge of the nightstand is 6 in. from the eastern edge of the bed.

The chest of drawers

There is a four-drawer chest of drawers along the north wall.

The chest of drawers is 3 ft wide; 1 ft, 8 in. deep, and 3 ft, 8 in. tall.

The back of the chest of drawers is flush against the north wall.

The eastern edge of the chest of drawers is 6 in. from the east wall.

The dresser

There is a six-drawer (two columns of three drawers) dresser on the east wall.

The dresser is 4 ft wide, 1 ft, 8 in. deep, and 3 ft, 8 in. tall.

The back of the dresser is flush against the east wall.

The northeast corner of the dresser is 4 ft, 6 in. from the northeast corner of the room.

The television stand

There is a television stand in the southwest corner of the room.

The television stand is 2 ft, 6 in. wide, 2 ft deep, and 2 ft, 8 in. high.

The back of the television stand is flush against the south wall.

The western edge of the television stand is 6 in. from the west wall of the room.

There is an area of dust on top of the television stand that is 2 ft, 3 in. wide and 1 ft, 2 in. deep. The area of dust is at an angle that indicates a television on the stand recently was canted toward the bed.

The Evidence

Baseline number one: using a protractor to ensure a 90° angle was obtained, a line bisecting the room from north to south was drawn, 7 ft from the northeast corner of the room and directly south from the southwest corner of nightstand number two (along its western edge). This is the baseline from which all items of evidence on the floor were measured. All items were measured at 90 degrees from the baseline.

The Pistol

There is a Colt 45 semiautomatic pistol on its left side with the barrel facing the chest of drawers.

The center of the weapon is 3 ft, 6 in. south of the nightstand corner.

The center of the weapon is 2 ft, 6 in. east of the baseline.

Footprint Number One

There is an apparent bloody shoeprint on the floor. The toe portion of the shoeprint points roughly from the bed to the entryway.

The center of the shoeprint is 6 ft, 8 in. south of the southwest corner of the second nightstand.

The center of the shoeprint is 2 ft, 1 in. east of the baseline.

Footprint Number Two

There is a second apparent bloody shoeprint on the floor. This shoeprint also points in the direction of the entryway.

The center of the shoeprint is 7 ft, 2 in. south of the southwest corner of the second nightstand.

The center of the shoeprint is 4 ft, 3 in. east of the baseline.

The Shell Casing

There is a shell casing on the floor near the foot of the bed.

The center of the shell casing is 6 ft, 2 in. south of the southwest corner of the second nightstand.

The center of the shell casing is 3 ft, 8 in. west of the baseline.

The Body

Baseline number two: for measurements of the head, the northern edge of the bed was used. Note that all blankets and sheets had been removed prior to crime scene examination.

The head

The apex of the head is 1 ft, 8 in. west of the northeast corner of the bed.
The apex of the head is 10 in. south of the baseline.

Baseline number three: for measurements of the remainder of the body, the eastern edge of the bed was used.

The neck

The center of the eastern edge of the neck is 2 ft, 1 in. from the northeast edge of the bed
The center of the eastern edge of the neck is 1 ft, 6 in. west of the baseline.

The left hand

The little finger of the left hand is 3 ft south of the northeast edge of the bed.
The little finger of the left hand is 10 in. west of baseline number three.

The left foot

    The base of the heel of the left foot is 5 ft, 2 in. south of the northeast edge of the bed.
    The base of the left heel is 1 ft, 4 in. west of the baseline.

The legs

    The legs are both straight out. The left heel is 3 in. across. There is a space of 8 in. between the left and right foot.

The right arm is on top of the body; therefore, no measurement could be made.

Document Your Activity

To complete this exercise, prepare a baseline measurement sketch on the page provided. Note that you will be able to document only the items described. Include all of the key elements on the sketch. Include appropriate measurements and document all items of furniture and evidence.

Exercise 1.8   Evidence Measurement Sketch: Baseline Method

NOTES

2

Photographic Documentation

In this section you will expand your knowledge of photography. Photography is another example of a nondestructive, minimally invasive processing technique at a crime scene. The importance of photographic documentation cannot be overstated. The old cliché is that a picture is worth a thousand words. This adage is particularly true in crime scene investigation. Whether the photographs are used for documentation of evidence, to verify alibis, to portray the crime scene in court, or for comparison in laboratory examinations, photographs are crucial to the successful resolution of a crime scene.

The exercises in this section consist of both paper-based and hands-on exercises. You have been provided with ample space to mount your photographs and with photography logs. Take your time and remember, crime scene photography is a once in a lifetime opportunity. If you miss the photograph, you can never get it back.

Exercise 2.1 Photography Terms

```
                    S L
                  W C E C
                 S Q U D M N
               H H H M A H Z B
              Y U L O U V I I J C
             V S A N B Y T Y C N B V
           J R G H B D D D T Q D X F F
          Z F V D N U A E P I E K W B I T
         P Q H T E W I T P R N O R M A L L L
        L D V E G S G C T T E E V P R J M H L C
       T E L E P H O T O N H E R X C N E P O W F V
      O L W L C P W P H O T O G R A P H Y L O G I L G
     N D A T P G Q O X M G X F I I S T O Z A E R L E A E
    D T L I T B B N J E W M L F E T L P U S N P A M A Q S Z
   A N G N I T E K C A R B G H I T B C K E R E B E S S S Y H A
  W R M G G R K P M V E C Z I E R U B A C E E D M P E I O W E
 H N H Q N A G B X U V D T G L N N G P P A D X R E L Z Y Q K
  I F V X Y D B U V S O F I Y D E F A Y D O B A R E M A C R O
 A L Y K X U C Y J C F W V W H H K I B I U T P N D B Z X Y T
A A O Y X E V A D D K I P B P Y H C U E P A S L Q Y C R B P
```

1. The size of the opening through which light penetrates to get to the film
2. When the subject of the photograph has bright light directly behind it
3. Adjusting the f/stop up and down from where the light meter indicates, enhancing the probability of a properly exposed photograph
4. The major portion of the camera system, holds the film, and the lens and flash are attached to it
5. The number of items in the photograph that are in sharp focus, looking "into" the photograph
6. Using a flash in daylight to enhance an area of deep shadow
7. The area within the camera body where the film actually sits
8. ASA 400, for example
9. A part of the camera system used to provide artificial light
10. That portion of the camera system that allows the subject of the photograph to come into focus
11. A type of lens for close-up photography
12. The lens used to portray a scene as it would look to the human eye
13. When too much light is allowed on the film
14. The document on which all of the key pieces of data about your photograph are recorded
15. The button depressed to take a photograph
16. The amount of time the lens is open, allowing light onto the film
17. A shutter speed of 1/500th is needed to accomplish this
18. A type of lens used for long-range photography
19. When not enough light is allowed on the film
20. A lens that allows a wider view than the normal eye can see

Practical Exercise 2.2: Basic Camera Operations

The purpose of this section is to familiarize you with the basics of camera operations. In this practical exercise, you will use the various functions on your camera to determine how shutter speed, depth of field, and focus all combine to document a crime scene. This will also enable you to learn the various functions of your camera in the manual mode. At the majority of crime scenes, you will be able to use your camera in the automatic or "point, focus, and shoot" mode. There are, however, many times when the situation mandates that you manipulate the data to obtain a certain view. For example, you may need to stop a vehicle in motion or blur out a crowd of onlookers at a crime scene. Being able to manipulate the information on your camera will enable you accomplish this. The most important aspect of camera operations for this exercise is the relationship between shutter speed and aperture to control the amount of light allowed in the camera. If you don't understand that relationship, it is unlikely you will be able to successfully document unusual situations.

During this practical exercise you will document your photographs on a Crime Scene Photography Log (Photo log).

Equipment Needed

1. A 35-mm quality camera (either film or digital) with a manually adjustable f/stop, shutter speed, and focal ring with a "normal" lens attached
2. Adequate color film or disc space to save images
3. Paper and pen

Complete the Exercises

Exercise 2.2.1: Shutter Speed Manipulation (7 Photographs)

You will need a static item to photograph in this exercise. This exercise will demonstrate to you how altering the amount of light that the camera allows in will alter the photograph. You will alter this amount of light by adjusting your shutter speed, thereby either increasing or decreasing the amount of light. Based upon your exercise, you may be able to determine times when it is appropriate to allow more or less light into the camera, thereby enhancing your photograph in some manner. For this exercise, pick an object that is about 15 ft away that clearly and totally fits in your view finder.

Document your photographs in the photo log as you take them.

Complete the following steps:

1. Focus on the object 15 ft in front of you and take a meter reading to determine the preferred camera settings in the manual mode; set your camera to those settings and take a photograph.
2. Without adjusting your f/stop or focus point, change your shutter speed to 1/30th and take a photograph.
3. Without adjusting your f/stop or focus point, change your shutter speed to 1/60th and take a photograph.

4. Without adjusting your f/stop or focus point, change your shutter speed to 1/125th and take a photograph.

5. Without adjusting your f/stop or focus point, change your shutter speed to 1/250th and take a photograph.

6. Without adjusting your f/stop or focus point, change your shutter speed to 1/500th and take a photograph.

7. Without adjusting your f/stop or focus point, change your shutter speed to 1/1000th and take a photograph.

Exercise 2.2.2: F/Stop Manipulation (7 Photographs)

This exercise will also demonstrate to you how altering the amount of light that the camera allows in will alter the photograph. This time you will alter the amount of light not by the length of time the shutter is open, but by the size of the aperture in the lens. Based upon your exercise, you may be able to determine times when it is appropriate to allow more or less light into the camera, thereby enhancing your photograph in some manner. What you will notice in this exercise is not only will the amount of light change the photograph quality, it will also alter the amount of photograph that is in clear focus, thus introducing you to depth of field. For this exercise, pick an object that is about 15 ft away that easily and totally fits in your view finder. You should use a different object than you used above so that you can clearly tell the photographs apart when you get them back from the developer.

Document your photographs in the photo log as you take them.

Complete the following steps:

1. Focus on the object fifteen feet in front of you and take a meter reading in the manual mode to determine the preferred camera settings. Take a photograph at those settings.

2. Without adjusting your shutter speed or focus point, change your f/stop to f/2.8 and take a photograph.

3. Without adjusting your shutter speed or focus point, change your f/stop to f/4 and take a photograph.

4. Without adjusting your shutter speed or focus point, change your f/stop to f/8 and take a photograph.

5. Without adjusting your shutter speed or focus point, change your f/stop to f/11 and take a photograph.

6. Without adjusting your shutter speed or focus point, change your f/stop to f/16 and take a photograph.

7. Without adjusting your shutter speed or focus point, change your f/stop to f/22 and take a photograph.

Note: If your camera is incapable of adjusting to each of the f/stops listed, merely adjust to as many f/stops as your particular camera will allow.

Exercise 2.2.3: Depth of Field/Focal Point (3 Photographs)

You will need three items in a row, about 3 ft apart (3 ft, 6 ft, and 9 ft from your lens). This exercise will demonstrate how the relationship of shutter speed to f/stop can be manipulated to either minimize or enlarge the amount of "depth" in the photograph that is in clear focus. This is what is meant by the term *depth of field*. Based upon your exercise, you may be able to determine times when it is appropriate to alter the depth of field.

Document your photographs in the photo log as you take them.

Complete the following steps:

1. Take up a position about 3 ft from the nearest object and hold your camera on the same horizontal plane as the objects to be photographed. Focus on the first object and take a meter reading to determine the preferred camera settings in the manual mode.
2. Manipulate the f/stop and shutter speed to obtain the lowest f/stop possible (as close to f/2.8 as possible). (You should have already had a lecture on the relationship of f/stop and shutter speed.)
3. Focus on the closest object and take a photograph.
4. Without adjusting the shutter speed or f/stop, focus on the second object and take a photograph.
5. Without adjusting the shutter speed or f/stop, focus on the third object and take a photograph.

Exercise 2.2.4: Depth of Field, F/Stop Manipulation (3 Photographs)

You will need three different items in a row, about 3 ft apart (3 ft, 6 ft, and 9 ft from your lens). This exercise will demonstrate to you how the relationship of shutter speed and f/stop can be manipulated to either minimize or enlarge the amount of "depth" in the photograph that is in clear focus. This is another aspect of depth of field. You will need to use the objects in the same manner as the above exercise. It is preferred that for this exercise, you use three different items so that you can easily tell the photographs apart when you get them back from development.

Document your photographs on the photo log as you take them.

Complete the following steps:

1. Take up a position about 3 ft from the nearest object and hold your camera on the same horizontal plane as the objects to be photographed. Focus on the second object and take a meter reading to determine the preferred camera settings in the manual mode.
2. Manipulate the f/stop and shutter speed to obtain the lowest f/stop possible (as close to f/2.8 as possible).
3. Refocus on the second object and take a photograph.
4. Without adjusting your focus point, adjust your camera as required so that you can obtain an f/stop of f/8 and take a photograph. (Remember that you will need to manipulate the shutter speed as well as the f/stop.)
5. Without adjusting your focus point, adjust your camera as required so that you get an f/stop of f/16 and take a photograph.

Exercise 2.2.5: Stopping Action via Shutter Speed (6 Photographs)

For this exercise, you will photograph a moving object at six separate shutter speeds. This will demonstrate for you the requirements for stopping action. You will need a continually moving object (persons running or cars passing perpendicular to you). This may be particularly useful in surveillance photography.

Document your photographs in the photo log as you take them.

Complete the following steps:

1. Determine what you wish to photograph and focus on the point where that object will pass in front of you.
2. Take a meter reading to determine the preferred camera settings in the manual mode.
3. Manipulate your camera to obtain the appropriate f/stop with a shutter speed of 1/30th, refocus and take a photograph.
4. Manipulate your camera to obtain the appropriate f/stop with a shutter speed of 1/125th, refocus and take a photograph.
5. Manipulate your camera to obtain the appropriate f/stop with a shutter speed of 1/250thth, refocus and take a photograph.
6. Manipulate your camera to obtain the appropriate f/stop with a shutter speed of 1/500th, refocus and take a photograph.

Document Your Activity

To complete this exercise, you must fill out the enclosed photography log completely. It is important to note that this form should have been completed contemporaneously with your photographs. If not completed in this manner, it is likely that data will be omitted.

After you receive the photographs back, number them in accordance with your photography log. Mount those photographs on the following pages and write two or three sentences concerning each photography exercise.

Photographic Log

Case Number_____Date/Time Begun_____

Detective Assigned Case_____

Photographer_____

Camera System _____Serial Number_____

Film Type_____ISO_____ # of Exposures on Roll _____

Lens(es) Used (Type/Serial Number) _____

Flash Information: Type/Serial Number:_____

Explanation of abbreviations: Camera position was eye level unless otherwise indicated.
DA = Directly above (perpendicular to subject of photograph)
N = Normal lens; M = Macro lens; W = Wide angle lens

Exposure #	Time	F/Stop	Shutter Speed	Distance	Description

Page _____ of _____ pages

Case Number_____ (Photographic Log Continued)

Exposure #	Time	F/Stop	Shutter Speed	Distance	Description

Basic Camera Operations Notes

On this page, you should answer the questions presented for this exercise. In your report, document how manipulation of the camera settings affects the quality of the photograph and when you feel each of these tasks would be of benefit.

You should see a difference in the quality of photograph in either how well the exposure is developed (over- or underexposed) or in the amount of photograph that is in sharp focus. What utility do these capabilities have for you?

NOTES

Exercise 2.2   Basic Camera Operations. Mount Your Work.

Technique_____

Photo number____   F/stop_____   Shutter Speed_____

Technique_____

Photo number____   F/stop_____   Shutter Speed_____

Technique_____

Photo number____   F/stop_____   Shutter Speed_____

Technique_____

Photo number____   F/stop_____   Shutter Speed_____

Exercise 2.2 (continued)   Basic Camera Operations. Mount Your Work.

Technique_____
Photo number____ F/stop____ Shutter Speed____

Technique_____
Photo number____ F/stop____ Shutter Speed____

Technique_____
Photo number____ F/stop____ Shutter Speed____

Technique_____
Photo number____ F/stop____ Shutter Speed____

Exercise 2.2 (continued)   Basic Camera Operations. Mount Your Work.

Technique_____

Photo number_____ F/stop_____ Shutter Speed_____

Technique_____

Photo number_____ F/stop_____ Shutter Speed_____

Technique_____

Photo number_____ F/stop_____ Shutter Speed_____

Technique_____

Photo number_____ F/stop_____ Shutter Speed_____

Exercise 2.2 (continued) **Basic Camera Operations. Mount Your Work.**

Technique_____

Photo number____ F/stop____ Shutter Speed____

Technique_____

Photo number____ F/stop____ Shutter Speed____

Technique_____

Photo number____ F/stop____ Shutter Speed____

Technique_____

Photo number____ F/stop____ Shutter Speed____

Exercise 2.2 (continued)   Basic Camera Operations. Mount Your Work.

Technique_____
Photo number____ F/stop_____ Shutter Speed_____

Technique_____
Photo number____ F/stop_____ Shutter Speed_____

Technique_____
Photo number____ F/stop_____ Shutter Speed_____

Technique_____
Photo number____ F/stop_____ Shutter Speed_____

Exercise 2.2 (continued)   Basic Camera Operations. Mount Your Work.

Technique_____
Photo number____ F/stop_____ Shutter Speed____

Technique_____
Photo number____ F/stop_____ Shutter Speed____

Technique_____
Photo number____ F/stop_____ Shutter Speed____

Technique_____
Photo number____ F/stop_____ Shutter Speed____

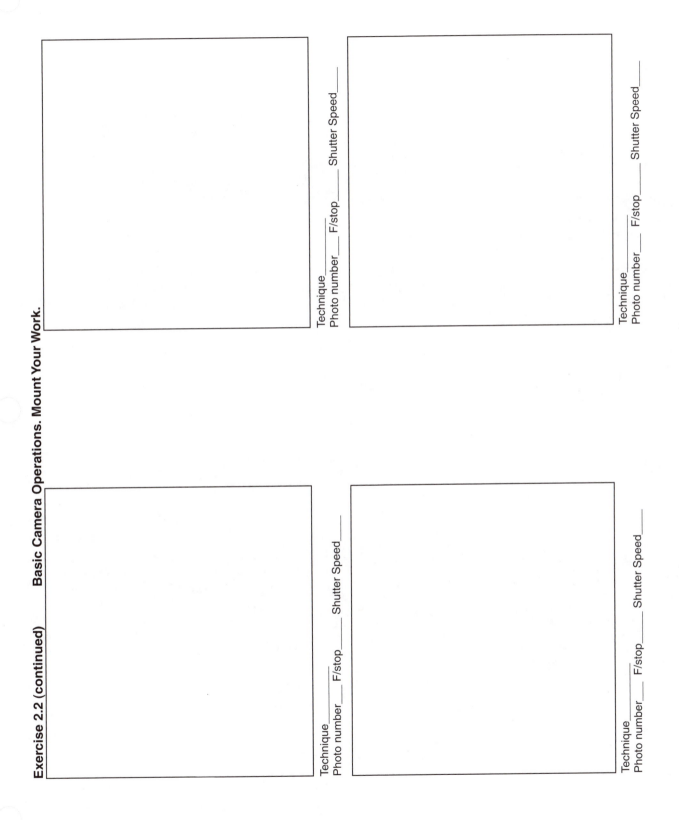

Exercise 2.2 (continued)   Basic Camera Operations. Mount Your Work.

Technique_____   F/stop_____   Shutter Speed_____
Photo number____

Technique_____   F/stop_____   Shutter Speed_____
Photo number____

Technique_____   F/stop_____   Shutter Speed_____
Photo number____

Technique_____   F/stop_____   Shutter Speed_____
Photo number____

Practical Exercise 2.3: Crime Scene Photography

The purpose of this section is to familiarize you with the basics of crime scene photo-documentation. This will include a 360° view of your crime scene, entrance photographs, and evidence photography.

In this practical exercise, you will use the automatic mode on your camera. You will obtain a meter reading and use the settings that your camera recommends for the lighting conditions you encounter.

During this practical exercise you will document your photographs on a Crime Scene Photography Log (Photo log). You should complete this photography log as you take the photographs.

Equipment Needed

1. A 35-mm quality camera (either film or digital) with a manually adjustable f/stop, shutter speed, and focal ring with a "normal" lens attached
2. Adequate film or disc space to save images
3. Tripod
4. Shutter release cable
5. A roll of pennies
6. A metal spoon or small hand shovel
7. Ruler
8. Paper and pencil

Complete the Exercises

Exercise 2.3.1: Outside 360° and Initial Entry Views (6 Photographs)

For this exercise you will photograph the exterior of a building. For purposes of the exercise, your goal is to completely encircle the building in no more than six photographs. Complete the following steps:

1. Take a meter reading to determine the preferred camera settings. Either set your camera on those settings or operate in the automatic mode.
2. Starting at the entry to the building which contains your "crime scene," take a photograph of the entryway. Successively walk around the building that contains the crime scene and expose photographs with the camera in the landscape orientation. Make sure you slightly overlap the photographs so that you will be able to record them in a "panoramic" view. Remember this is merely documentation of the crime scene and not evidence. Because of this fact, you can back up to a much greater distance to ensure you get the entire building in the fewest number of photographs.

Exercise 2.3.2: Inside 360° View (5 Photographs)

For this exercise you will need an interior room which contains at least three items of "evidence" from your crime scene.

1. Take a meter reading to determine the preferred camera settings for the light conditions in the room and set your camera on those settings.

2. Starting at the entry to your "crime scene," take a photograph of the floor to document whether or not evidence is present. Next, with your camera in the landscape position, walk around the crime scene and expose photographs. Make sure you slightly overlap the photographs so that you will be able to record them in a "panoramic" view. Remember that the purpose of these photographs is merely documentation of the crime scene and not documentation of evidence. Although items of evidence will still be included in the photographs, they are not the primary focus of the photographs.

Exercise 2.3.3: Evidence Photography (12 Photographs)

For this exercise you will photograph two different items of "evidence" from your inside 360° view photographs. You will take two additional evidence photographs in different orientations. This exercise will enable you to take evidence photographs in four different situations which each present unique challenges.

For each item of evidence, you will take three photographs. Those photographs are referred to as (1) an evidence-establishing photograph, (2) an evidence close-up photograph without scale, and (3) an evidence close-up photograph with scale.

Evidence Item 1

This should be a relatively flat item such as a piece of paper or a footprint on the floor.

1. Take a meter reading to determine the preferred camera settings; set your camera on those settings.

2. Take an evidence-establishing photograph. This is a photograph of the item of evidence in relation to a fixed item in the room. Ideally, you will position yourself approximately five feet from the evidence and include the item of evidence and some other item in the room that will orient the position of the evidence. Focus on the item of evidence, not the surrounding items.

3. Take an evidence close-up photograph without a scale. This is a photograph of just the item of evidence. Remember to get close enough to completely fill the frame of your viewfinder with the item. Focus on the item of evidence, and ensure your camera is perpendicular to the item being photographed.

4. Take an evidence close-up photograph, with scale. This photograph should look virtually the same as the previous photograph, only with a scale inserted. With your camera in the same position as the evidence close-up without scale, insert the scale and take the photograph.

Evidence Item 2

For this item of evidence use an item that has height, for example, a book. Your actions are essentially the same, with the exception of the scale.

1. Take a meter reading to determine the preferred camera settings; set your camera on those settings.

2. Take an evidence-establishing photograph, as described above, of evidence item number two.

3. Move in toward the item of evidence to take the evidence close-up photograph without a scale as described above. Remember to orient your camera perpendicular to the evidence.

4. Next, take an evidence close-up photograph, with scale. Your challenge now is to remember that the item now has height associated with it. You must raise the scale to the same plane as your evidence. To accomplish this, you can use any number of objects. One method is to keep a roll of pennies, so that you can build a tower on either side of the ruler to raise your ruler to the level of the item. The process is that you gently build a tower of coins or other metallic disks.

5. Stack the coins one on top of another until the stack reaches the height of the evidence. Repeat this process so that you have two towers.

6. Place the ruler on top of the stacks. Refocus on the subject of the photograph, ensuring that you completely fill the frame with the subject of the photograph and the scale inserted, and expose the photograph.

Evidence Item 3

For this item you will not be able to photograph inside your interior crime scene. The technique here is to have an object that has depth, for example, a footprint in soft soil. Your actions are essentially the same, with the exception of the scale. For this item of evidence, you will need to locate an item of evidence outside.

1. Take a meter reading to determine the preferred camera settings; set your camera on those settings.

2. Focus on the item of evidence and take the evidence-establishing photograph as described above.

3. Next, you will move into the item of evidence and take an evidence close-up photograph without a scale as described above. Remember to orient your camera perpendicular to the item of evidence.

4. Take the evidence close-up photograph, with scale. Your challenge is to remember that the item now has depth and you must lower the scale to the same plane as your evidence. To accomplish this, you can use any number of objects. One method is to keep a spoon in your camera kit. With your spoon, gently dig a small trench next to your item of evidence to lower the ruler to the level of the item. When you have dug a small trench, set the ruler in place adjacent to the item of evidence. Refocus on the evidence, making sure you include your ruler, and take the photograph.

Evidence Item 4

For this item, use an object that is perpendicular to the ground, such as a bloody palm print on a window. Your actions are essentially the same, with the exception of the scale.

1. Take a meter reading to determine the preferred camera settings; set your camera on those settings.

2. Take the evidence-establishing photograph as described above.

3. Take the evidence close-up photograph without a scale as described above.

4. Take the evidence close-up photograph, with scale. Your challenge is to remember that the item is now on a vertical plane. To this point, all of your evidence photographs have been on a horizontal plane. You cannot use the ground on which to set your scale. You must keep the scale on the same plane as your evidence. To accomplish this, mount your camera on a tripod and attach the shutter release cable. Focus on the item of evidence.

5. Stand adjacent to the item of evidence, and hold the scale flat on the surface that has the evidence.

6. Using your shutter release cable, expose the photograph.

Document Your Activity

To complete this exercise, you must fill out the enclosed photography log. As a reminder, you should have filled out the photography log as you exposed all of the photographs.

After you receive the photographs back, number them in accordance with your photography log. Mount those photographs on the following pages and write a short report concerning each photography exercise. Include in your report how overlapping of the photographs is important. Also, discuss the importance of evidence-establishing and evidence close-up photographs. Does the use of the scale in the evidence close-up photograph present any additional challenges? Finally, mention how manipulation of the camera setting affects the quality of the photograph.

Photographic Log

Case Number_____Date/Time Begun_____

Detective Assigned Case_____

Photographer_____

Camera System _____Serial Number_____

Film Type_____ISO_____ # of Exposures on Roll _____

Lens(es) Used (Type/Serial Number) _____

Flash Information: Type/Serial Number:_____

Explanation of abbreviations: Camera position was eye level unless otherwise indicated.
DA = Directly above (perpendicular to subject of photograph)
N = Normal lens; M = Macro lens; W = Wide angle lens

Exposure #	Time	F/Stop	Shutter Speed	Distance	Description

Page _____ of _____ pages

Crime Scene Processing Laboratory Manual and Workbook

Case Number_____ (Photographic Log Continued)

Exposure #	Time	F/Stop	Shutter Speed	Distance	Description

NOTES

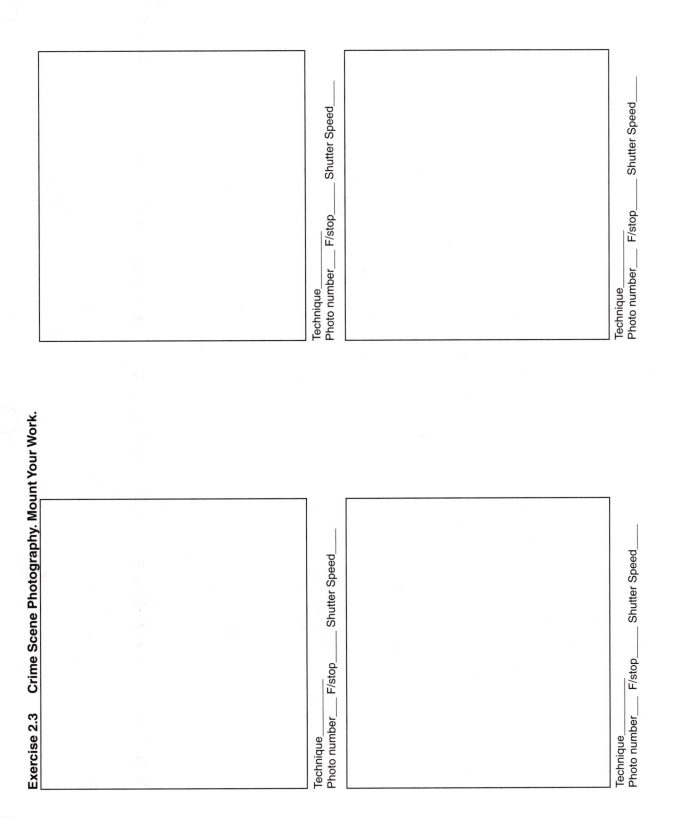

Exercise 2.3 Crime Scene Photography. Mount Your Work.

Technique_____
Photo number_____ F/stop_____ Shutter Speed_____

Technique_____
Photo number_____ F/stop_____ Shutter Speed_____

Technique_____
Photo number_____ F/stop_____ Shutter Speed_____

Technique_____
Photo number_____ F/stop_____ Shutter Speed_____

Exercise 2.3 (continued)　　Crime Scene Photography. Mount Your Work.

Technique_____ F/stop_____ Shutter Speed_____
Photo number_____

Technique_____ F/stop_____ Shutter Speed_____
Photo number_____

Technique_____ F/stop_____ Shutter Speed_____
Photo number_____

Technique_____ F/stop_____ Shutter Speed_____
Photo number_____

Exercise 2.3 (continued)   **Crime Scene Photography. Mount Your Work.**

Technique _____
Photo number _____ F/stop _____ Shutter Speed _____

Technique _____
Photo number _____ F/stop _____ Shutter Speed _____

Technique _____
Photo number _____ F/stop _____ Shutter Speed _____

Technique _____
Photo number _____ F/stop _____ Shutter Speed _____

Exercise 2.3 (continued)   **Crime Scene Photography. Mount Your Work.**

Technique_____

Photo number_____ F/stop_____ Shutter Speed_____

Technique_____

Photo number_____ F/stop_____ Shutter Speed_____

Technique_____

Photo number_____ F/stop_____ Shutter Speed_____

Technique_____

Photo number_____ F/stop_____ Shutter Speed_____

Exercise 2.3 (continued)   **Crime Scene Photography. Mount Your Work.**

Technique_____
Photo number_____ F/stop_____ Shutter Speed_____

Technique_____
Photo number_____ F/stop_____ Shutter Speed_____

Technique_____
Photo number_____ F/stop_____ Shutter Speed_____

Technique_____
Photo number_____ F/stop_____ Shutter Speed_____

Exercise 2.3 (continued)   Crime Scene Photography. Mount Your Work.

Technique_____ F/stop_____ Shutter Speed____
Photo number____

Technique_____ F/stop_____ Shutter Speed____
Photo number____

Technique_____ F/stop_____ Shutter Speed____
Photo number____

Technique_____ F/stop_____ Shutter Speed____
Photo number____

Practical Exercise 2.4: Flash Photography

The purpose of this section is to familiarize you not only with the capabilities of your flash unit, but also with the various techniques that can be used with a flash to enhance crime scene documentation.

In this exercise, you will use the flash from your camera in several different scenarios to determine what your flash is capable of and when it is appropriate to employ your flash at a crime scene in various light conditions.

During this practical exercise you will document your photographs on a Crime Scene Photography Log (Photographic log).

Equipment Needed

1. A 35-mm quality camera (either film or digital) with a manually adjustable f/stop, shutter speed, and focal ring with a "normal" lens attached
2. Adequate film or disc space to save images
3. A flash synchronized to your camera that can be manually fired
4. A shutter release cable
5. A tripod
6. An assistant
7. At least 10 members of your class or 10 differently colored cones
8. A strong flashlight or vehicle spotlight

Complete the Exercises

Completely fill out your photography log as you accomplish the various exercises.

Exercise 2.4.1: Capabilities of Your Flash (10 Photographs)
One of the most common errors in nighttime crime scene documentation is improper use of the flash. Oftentimes the crime scene technicians are unfamiliar with the capabilities and limitations of the flash attachment to their cameras. In this exercise, you will determine the width and depth capabilities of your flash.

Exercise 2.4.1.1: Width Capability of the Flash (5 Photographs)
To accomplish this exercise you will need either 10 fellow students or 10 differently colored cones that you can line up in a horizontal row, each three feet apart. This exercise will enable you to determine the width of coverage your camera will provide in a flash situation.

1. Line the students or the cones in a straight row, 3 ft apart to give a consistent distance for your photographs.

2. Lay out a tape measure 30 ft long, perpendicular with the center student or cone.

3. Focus on the center student in the row.

4. Set your camera on f/8 (this is a good midrange depth of field).

5. Synchronize your shutter speed with your flash.

6. Take a position 10 feet from the center student, focus on the center student, and expose a photograph.

7. Move to a position 15 ft from the center student, refocus, and expose a photograph.

8. Move to a position 20 ft from the center student, refocus, and expose a photograph.

9. Move to a position 25 ft from the center student, refocus, and expose a photograph.

10. Move to a position 30 ft from the center student, refocus, and expose a photograph.

Exercise 2.4.1.2: Depth Capability of Your Flash (5 Photographs)

To accomplish this exercise you will need either 10 fellow students or 10 differently colored cones lined up in a vertical row, each 3 ft apart. This exercise will enable you to determine the how far "into" your photograph you can get good coverage with your flash.

1. Line the students or the cones in a straight row, three feet apart to give a consistent distance for your photographs. Have each student stand 1 ft to the left of the student in front of him/her. If you are using differently colored cones, stagger them slightly off center so that you can see the depth of the cones. This action will ensure you can tell how deep into the photograph you can clearly see.

2. Lay out a tape measure 30 ft long, perpendicular with the front student or cone.

3. Set your camera on f/8 (this is a good midrange depth of field).

4. Synchronize your shutter speed with your flash.

5. Take up a position 5 ft from the first student or cone, focus on that object, synchronize your flash, and expose a photograph.

6. Take up a position 10 ft from the first student or cone, focus on that object, synchronize your flash, and expose a photograph.

7. Take up a position 15 ft from the first student or cone, focus on that object, synchronize your flash, and expose a photograph.

8. Take up a position 20 ft from the first student or cone, focus on that object, synchronize your flash, and expose a photograph.

9. Take up a position 30 ft from the first student or cone, focus on that object, synchronize your flash, and expose a photograph.

Exercise 2.4.2: Fill Flash (4 Photographs)

In crime scene photography, we cannot control the light conditions. While an ideal condition is a slightly cloudy day, we must be able to document our crime scene in extremely bright circumstances.

When a backlight condition exists, you can employ your flash to make your image identifiable. Not only may you find yourself in a backlight situation, but frequently evidence is located in an area of heavy shadow, which may not be visible to a camera without your help.

Exercise 2.4.2.1: Backlight Situations (2 Photographs)

1. In a very bright sunlight situation, place a fellow student directly between you and the sun.
2. Place yourself 5 ft from the subject of your photograph and focus on that object.
3. Take meter reading on your camera. Set your camera to those readings and expose a photograph without the benefit of a flash.
4. Using the same camera settings, attach your flash, synchronize your flash with your camera, refocus on the subject, and expose another photograph with the flash.

When you get these photographs back from development, you should be able to see a difference in clarity of your subject when you use the flash in this situation.

Exercise 2.4.2.2: Heavy Shadow Situations (2 Photographs)

In a very bright sunlight situation, place an item of "evidence" (such as a book, a knife, or a gun) in an area of heavy shadow (near the edge of the shadow/sun line). This exercise will enable you to determine the benefits you may obtain from use of a flash in daylight situations.

1. Stand completely in the sunlight, focus on the item from about 5 ft away, and take a meter reading. Set your camera to those readings, refocus on the subject, and expose a photograph without the benefit of a flash.
2. Using the same camera settings, attach your flash, synchronize your flash with your camera, refocus, and expose the same photograph with the flash.

Exercise 2.4.3: Painting with Light (6 Photographs)

Just as you cannot control the lighting conditions of a crime scene, neither can you control the size of the crime scene you are tasked with photographing. As you have learned, we are limited in the amount of area that can be covered with traditional flash photography. Fortunately, there are other methods of introducing light into our crime scene. If you use these other techniques, you may be able to document a much deeper or much wider area than your flash can adequately cover. One technique that you can use is called painting with light. You employ painting with light when you need to complete photo-documentation of a crime scene in darkness. Examples of this situation would be a building that has lost electricity or in a field at night. Because these photographs are one in a million, you will also use the technique known as bracketing to enhance the probability that the photographs will come out properly. You can accomplish painting with light either with a detached flash or with a strong spotlight.

Exercise 2.4.3.1: Detached Flash (3 Photographs)
Detached flash is the preferred method when you have a crime scene that has a greater depth than your flash is capable of. To accomplish this exercise, in a very low light condition, create a crime scene that is about 50 ft "deep" and rather narrow (such as you might find with skid marks at a traffic accident).

1. Place your camera on its tripod.
2. Attach the shutter release cable.
3. Set your camera's shutter speed to "B" (bulb).
4. Set your f/stop to f/8.
5. Using a spotlight or other strong constant light, illuminate the primary subject of your photograph, and focus on that subject. Then turn off the light.

Based upon your results in prior flash exercises, you know how much coverage you can get with one flash. You must determine at what points in your crime scene you must provide light. The object is to plot out positions that will provide 100% coverage of the crime scene between the main subject and the camera position. Plot out those points and determine the most direct path from one point to the other.

1. Have your assistant walk from spot to spot and practice his route so that he can quickly traverse the distance when you take the photograph.
2. After your assistant has practiced his route, have him go back to the farthest spot and hold the flash out in front of his body, pointed toward the subject of the photograph.
3. Place a clipboard or other item in front of the lens and depress the shutter release cable. Lock the shutter in the open position.
4. While your assistant is at the first spot (closest to the deepest part of the scene) move the clipboard away from the lens.
5. Instruct the assistant to manually fire the flash.
6. Cover the lens with the clipboard. Care must be taken not to actually touch the lens or camera body with the clipboard. You are merely attempting to keep excess ambient light from penetrating the camera lens while the assistant moves to the next spot.
7. Have the assistant move to each successive predetermined spot and repeat the above steps until you have worked all the way back to the camera from the scene. Normally you will need about four different flashes in the photograph to properly expose the crime scene.
8. Release the shutter release cable.

Now you will bracket the photograph. As a review, bracketing is merely altering the amount of light that enters the camera, thereby changing the exposure of your image. By altering the f/stop you will modify the amount of light that is allowed into the camera, which will alter the exposure of the photograph. Because a real crime scene is a once in a lifetime photograph, you must take extra steps to ensure that you get a good photograph.

1. Change your f/stop to f/5.6 and repeat the above exercise on that setting.
2. Change your f/stop to f/11 and repeat the above exercise on that setting.

Exercise 2.4.3.2: Use of a Spotlight for Tall One-Dimensional Crime Scenes (3 Photographs)
The use of a spotlight is the preferred method when you have a crime scene that has either greater width or height than your flash is capable of. To accomplish this exercise, in a very low light condition, create a crime scene that is relatively one dimensional (such as the side of a darkened building, yet taller and wider than your flash can cover).

1. Place your camera on its tripod.
2. Attach the shutter release cable.
3. Set your camera's shutter speed to "B" (bulb).
4. Set your f/stop to f/8.
5. Shine a steady light on the center of the subject of your photograph and properly focus the camera. After you have focused, turn off the light.
6. Depress the shutter release cable. Lock the shutter in the open position.
7. With either a powerful flashlight or a vehicle spotlight, slowly "paint" the side of the building, as if you were painting a wall with a roller. Slowly cover the entire building, both horizontally and vertically.
8. After you have "painted" the scene, release the shutter release cable.

Now you will bracket the photograph. By altering the f/stop you will modify the amount of light that is allowed into the camera, which will alter the exposure of the photograph. Because a real crime scene is a once in a lifetime photograph, you must take extra steps to ensure that you get a good photograph.

1. Change your f/stop to f/5.6 and repeat the above exercise.
2. Change your f/stop to f/11 and repeat the above exercise.

Exercise 2.4.4: Heavy Shadow Situations without a Flash (2 Photographs)

Many times we may find ourselves at a crime scene that has heavy shadows as well as bright sunlight. In these situations, items of evidence are likely in both areas and must be documented so that all persons involved in the investigation can accurately see everything in the crime scene. Your eyes are capable of automatically altering the information you receive to accurately see the items in shadows even though you are in sunlight. Your camera cannot do this, so you must manipulate the information the camera receives and over- or underexpose certain portions of the crime scene. You accomplish this through exposing two photographs of the same scene, from the same location, using different settings.

1. Find a location that is heavily shadowed and stand on the edge of that location, but remain completely in the sun.

2. Look with your eyes at something deep in the shadows. When you have that object in focus, focus your camera on it and take a meter reading while your camera is in bright sunlight.

3. Set your camera on those settings.

4. Refocus on the object and expose a photograph using the recommended settings.

5. Now walk up to the subject of your photograph and take a meter reading with your camera completely in the shadows.

6. Return to your original position, refocus on the object and expose a photograph of the same object from the same spot. Ensure your camera is set to the settings you obtained while completely immersed in the shadows.

The result of this exercise is that in your first photograph, the brightly lit area will be properly exposed and the subject will be underexposed. In the second photograph, the sunny area will be overexposed and the subject in the shadows will be properly exposed.

Document Your Activity

To complete this exercise, you must fill out the enclosed photography log completely. It is important to note that this form should be completed contemporaneously with your photographs. If not completed in this manner, it is likely that data will be omitted.

After you receive the photographs back, number them in accordance with your photography log. Mount those photographs on the following pages and write two or three sentences concerning each photography exercise. In your written report, document how manipulation of the flash affects the quality of the photograph and when you feel each of these methods would be of benefit. You also should be able, based on your photographs, to clearly document the capabilities of your flash unit.

Photographic Log

Case Number_____Date/Time Begun_____

Detective Assigned Case_____

Photographer_____

Camera System _____Serial Number_____

Film Type_____ISO_____ # of Exposures on Roll _____

Lens(es) Used (Type/Serial Number) _____

Flash Information: Type/Serial Number:_____

Explanation of abbreviations: Camera position was eye level unless otherwise indicated.
DA = Directly above (perpendicular to subject of photograph)
N = Normal lens; M = Macro lens; W = Wide angle lens

Exposure #	Time	F/Stop	Shutter Speed	Distance	Description

Page _____ of _____ pages

Case Number_____ (Photographic Log Continued)

Exposure #	Time	F/Stop	Shutter Speed	Distance	Description

Flash Photography Notes

On this page, you should answer the questions presented for this exercise. In your report, document how manipulation of the camera settings affects the quality of the photograph and when you feel each of these methods would be of benefit. Were you able to determine the capabilities of your flash? Can you determine a time when you may be able to employ fill flash techniques?

NOTES

Exercise 2.4   Flash Photography. Mount Your Work.

Technique _____ F/stop _____ Shutter Speed _____
Photo number _____

Technique _____ F/stop _____ Shutter Speed _____
Photo number _____

Technique _____ F/stop _____ Shutter Speed _____
Photo number _____

Technique _____ F/stop _____ Shutter Speed _____
Photo number _____

Exercise 2.4 (continued)   Flash Photography. Mount Your Work.

Technique_____
Photo number_____ F/stop_____ Shutter Speed_____

Technique_____
Photo number_____ F/stop_____ Shutter Speed_____

Technique_____
Photo number_____ F/stop_____ Shutter Speed_____

Technique_____
Photo number_____ F/stop_____ Shutter Speed_____

Exercise 2.4 (continued)   Flash Photography. Mount Your Work.

Technique _____   F/stop _____   Shutter Speed _____
Photo number _____

Technique _____   F/stop _____   Shutter Speed _____
Photo number _____

Technique _____   F/stop _____   Shutter Speed _____
Photo number _____

Technique _____   F/stop _____   Shutter Speed _____
Photo number _____

Exercise 2.4 (continued)   Flash Photography. Mount Your Work.

Technique_____ F/stop_____ Shutter Speed____
Photo number___

Technique_____ F/stop_____ Shutter Speed____
Photo number___

Technique_____ F/stop_____ Shutter Speed____
Photo number___

Technique_____ F/stop_____ Shutter Speed____
Photo number___

Exercise 2.4 (continued)   Flash Photography. Mount Your Work.

Technique_____ F/stop_____ Shutter Speed_____
Photo number____

Technique_____ F/stop_____ Shutter Speed_____
Photo number____

Technique_____ F/stop_____ Shutter Speed_____
Photo number____

Technique_____ F/stop_____ Shutter Speed_____
Photo number____

Exercise 2.4 (continued)   **Flash Photography. Mount Your Work.**

Technique_____
Photo number____ F/stop_____ Shutter Speed_____

Technique_____
Photo number____ F/stop_____ Shutter Speed_____

Technique_____
Photo number____ F/stop_____ Shutter Speed_____

Technique_____
Photo number____ F/stop_____ Shutter Speed_____

3

Fingerprint Evidence

In this section you will be introduced to fingerprints. They are usually the most common evidence at a crime scene; however, they are frequently overlooked. The proper search for, development of, and collection of latent fingerprint evidence will indelibly link a person to the crime scene. While this individual evidence is direct evidence of presence at a crime scene, it may not be direct evidence of guilt. This fact can only be proven or disproven through thorough and accurate investigation.

Fingerprint development is an extremely destructive investigative technique. For this reason, proper photographic documentation is imperative. Although a photographic section has not been included in this series of exercises, you absolutely must photograph your developed latent impressions both without and with a scale. As you will find, some of your impressions will look very good to you when you develop them; however, they may be less than desirable when you attempt to lift them. Hopefully any failures you may experience in practice will emphasize the importance of your photographs.

You will conduct only the most basic fingerprint development techniques in this section. These exercises consist of powder techniques and cyanoacrylate ester (superglue) development. While a large number of chemical methods for developing fingerprints are available, a crime scene investigator must be able to deftly wield a fingerprint brush. These exercises will teach you how to accomplish this task.

The exercises in this section are both paper-based and hands-on.

You have been provided with ample pages to mount your fingerprint lifts, and like the other parts of this book, this section when completed should be removed and mounted in your three ring binder for future reference. Note that enough pages for mounting have been provided for two or three attempts at lifts.

Exercise 3.1 Fingerprints

```
                    R
                  A E G
                F V T B U
              R J B F W R M
            J E I V I Y E L X
          F Z H Q D L A T E N T
        N O I T A C R U F I B N P
      O D E M A G N E T I C N E O T
    A I Q G Q E O R B L L M G T V Q N
  M D H C P H F B F B P E J U A J R B V
S B A N P L U D O E U L G R E P U S F F A
  H T P S N I Z H C R A N U X Y V J O W
    M F D M Y L O O P S I I G T Z Q P
      Y Z U T S H I K T H J X W H T
        E M H W E O Q I B G T V Q
          V M D W E F C D R U H
            X J N C L A I T Q
              Z U U U A V J
                O O T H U
                  M K T
                    O
```

1. The fingerprint pattern that rises in the center and falls off on both sides
2. When a ridge in an impression splits in two
3. A type of brush used primarily with fluorescent powder
4. A plastic lifting material with a clear cover
5. An impression not visible to the naked eye
6. The most common fingerprint pattern
7. Impression development material made of ferrous material
8. An impression that is visible to the naked eye
9. An impression in a soft substance such as butter
10. A lifting material that is pliable and can be used for items such as a door knob
11. Cyanoacrylate ester
12. The fingerprint pattern in a circle

Practical Exercise 3.2: Basic Latent Impression Development with All-Purpose Powder

The purpose of this section is to identify, develop, and lift latent impressions using traditional powders.

In this practical exercise, you will compare traditional powders. Traditional all-purpose powder works on all nonporous surfaces. This powder is sometimes mistakenly called "Volcanic" or "Volcano" powder. Those terms actually refer to a brand of all-purpose powder. You will use both black and white all-purpose powders. You will apply the powder with the three different types of brushes. The brushes you will use are a camel's hair brush, a fiberglass brush, and a feather brush. After you have developed the impressions, you will lift them using hinge lifters, rubber lifters, and lifting tape. As a result of this exercise, you should come up with a combination of brush, powder, and lifter that works best for you. Remember, the person working next to you may find a different combination that works for him/her.

At the conclusion of the practical exercise, you will prepare a written report that will identify your steps taken and your results, and will compare the various methods. Finally, in your report, determine which method you prefer and why.

Equipment Needed

1. Adequate nonporous smooth surface materials to develop impressions (red-colored plastic plates work well)
2. Black all-purpose powder
3. White all-purpose powder
4. Two Camel's hair brushes
5. Two Fiberglass brushes
6. Two Feather brushes
7. Clear-back hinge lifters
8. White-back hinge lifters
9. Black-back hinge lifters
10. White-back rubber lifters
11. Black-back rubber lifters
12. Lifting tape, 2 in. wide

Complete the Exercises

Exercise 3.2.1: Black All-Purpose Powder

In this portion of the exercise, you will use black all-purpose powder to develop impressions. Black powder works well on light-colored surfaces.

Exercise 3.2.1.1: Camel's Hair Brush

1. Examine the surface for impressions. Ensure the surface will allow a good contrast for black powder. Use oblique lighting techniques to attempt to locate a latent impression. You may not find a latent impression, but an oblique light can help limit the areas you process for impressions.

2. Prepare a shallow "dish" out of a piece of paper by folding up the sides, to hold your powder.

3. Place a small amount of black all-purpose powder in the paper dish (this makes loading your brush much easier).

4. Dip your camel's hair brush into the powder and fill the brush with powder, both on the fringes and in the center of the brush.

5. Tap the handle of the brush on your finger to get excess powder off the brush.

6. Use a very gentle touch to lightly "paint" the powder over the impression. Use care not to destroy the print with the brush.

7. When the impression has developed to the point that good ridge detail is visible, stop development and move on to lifting the impression.

White-Back or Clear Hinge Lifter

1. Open your white-back or clear hinge lifter and apply the lifter from the open end toward the hinge portion of the lift. Carefully rub air pockets out toward the edges of the lifter with your finger as you press down.

2. Lift the hinge lifter and carefully close.

3. Mark your lifter in accordance with departmental guidelines.

White-Back Rubber Lifter

1. Repeat the above steps but lift the impression with a white-back rubber lifter. The lifting technique is the same.

Clear Lifting Tape

Repeat the above steps but lift the impression with a roll of clear lifting tape. This lifting technique varies slightly from hinge and rubber lifters. When you are ready to lift, follow these steps:

1. If you are on a horizontal surface, pull an ample amount of tape off the roll so that you can hold each end above the impression.

2. Hold the tape in a "U" shape and allow the center of the tape to touch the impression. Then gently press down, while at the same time working out any air bubbles.

3. If you are on a vertical surface, use gravity to your advantage and let the weight of the tape roll assist you in eliminating bubbles. In this case, you would apply the tape above the impression and work your way down the tape until the impression is completely covered.

4. Cut the tape and adhere it to a clean clear piece of acetate (such as a clear document protector).

5. Mark the lift in accordance with your departmental policy.

Exercise 3.2.1.2: Fiberglass Brush

A fiberglass brush works much the same as a camel's hair brush, with the exception of the manner of applying the powder. While a camel's hair brush acts more like a paint brush, a fiberglass brush will flare out and allow you to apply the powder.

After you have discovered an area you wish to process for impressions, you can use the same powder dish and powder you prepared above.

1. Dip your fiberglass brush into the powder, filling the brush with powder, both on the fringes and in the center of the brush.
2. Tap the handle of the brush on your finger to get excess powder off the brush.
3. Grip the brush between your thumb and forefinger and gently spin the brush in your fingers. This will cause the fiberglass bristles to flare out, which is how you will paint the impression
4. Using a spinning motion lightly touch the impression, using care to lightly touch the impression with only the extreme edges of the bristles. You can use either the outer edges that have flared out or the center bristles that are also full of powder. As before, you must take care not to destroy the print with the brush.
5. When the impression has developed to the point that good ridge detail is visible, stop development and move on to lifting the impression.

White-Back or Clear Hinge Lifters

1. After you have developed the impression, use a clear or white-back hinge lifter to lift the impression, as described above.

White-Back Rubber Lifters

1. Repeat the above steps but lift the impression with a white-back rubber lifter, as described above.

Clear Lifting Tape

1. Repeat the above steps but lift the impression with a roll of clear lifting tape as described above.

Exercise 3.2.1.3: Feather Brush

A feather brush works much the same as other brushes, although you will see that the feather brush is much more sensitive. The technique used to apply powder with a feather brush is much the same as with a camel's hair brush.

1. Repeat the same steps you used above regarding locating and preparing to develop a latent impression.
2. Load your feather brush with powder from your paper dish and tap off the excess as previously described.
3. Apply the feather brush to the impression in a light "painting" motion to develop the impression.
4. After the impression has been developed, move on to lifting the impression.

White-Back or Clear Hinge Lifters

1. After you have developed the impression, use a clear or white-back hinge lifter to lift the impression, as described above.

White-Back Rubber Lifters

1. Repeat the above steps but lift the impression with a white-back rubber lifter, as described above.

Clear Lifting Tape

1. Repeat the above steps but lift the impression with a roll of clear lifting tape as descibed above.

Exercise 3.2.2: White All-Purpose Powder

In this portion of the exercise you will use white all-purpose powder instead of black. The use of white powder would be indicated on very dark surfaces where black powders would not provide the contrast required to observe ridge detail.

All of your actions in this section are the same as they were for the black powder. The only difference is that you will use white powder in lieu of black. Remember that you will need to create a new dish for your white powder and will need three different clean brushes, one of each type.

Exercise 3.2.2.1: Camel's Hair Brush

1. Repeat the steps described in the section for black powder with your camel's hair brush. Follow those directions to develop the impression with white powder.

Clear- or Black-Back Hinge Lifters

1. Repeat the above steps but lift the impression with a clear- or black-back hinge lifter. The lifting technique is the same as described above.

Black-Back Rubber Lifters

1. Repeat the above steps but lift the impression with a black-back rubber lifter. The lifting technique is the same as described above.

Clear Lifting Tape

1. Repeat the above steps but lift the impression with a roll of clear lifting tape. The lifting technique is the same as described above.

Exercise 3.2.2.2: Fiberglass Brush

1. Repeat the steps described in the section for black powder with your fiberglass brush. Follow those directions to develop the impression with white powder.

Clear- or Black-Back Hinge Lifters

1. Repeat the above steps but lift the impression with a clear- or black-back hinge lifter. The lifting technique is the same as described above.

Black-Back Rubber Lifters

1. Repeat the above steps but lift the impression with a black-back rubber lifter. The lifting technique is the same as described above.

Clear Lifting Tape

1. Repeat the above steps but lift the impression with a roll of clear lifting tape. The lifting technique is the same as described above.

Exercise 3.2.2.3: Feather Brush

1. Repeat the steps described in the section for black powder with your feather brush. Follow those directions to develop the impression with white powder.

Clear or Black-Back Hinge Lifters

1. Repeat the above steps but lift the impression with a clear- or black-back hinge lifter. The lifting technique is the same as described above.

Black-Back Rubber Lifters

1. Repeat the above steps but lift the impression with a black-back rubber lifter. The lifting technique is the same as described above.

Clear Lifting Tape

1. Repeat the above steps but lift the impression with a roll of clear lifting tape. The lifting technique is the same as described above.

Document Your Activity

To complete this exercise, you need to document your findings. Include factors such as ease of use, time involved, quality of the print, or if the print is reversed. Did you find any one brush that worked better than another? Did one clean up better than another? Is there a large amount of clean up required? Finally, take a position as to your favorite combinations of powder, brush, and lifting material and defend your position.

Mount your impressions on the following pages. Room has been provided for two lifts to be mounted in each box.

NOTES

Exercise 3.2   Basic All-Purpose Powder Development. Mount Your Work.

Technique_____

Technique_____

Technique_____

Technique_____

Technique_____

Technique_____

Exercise 3.2 (continued)   **Basic All-Purpose Powder Development. Mount Your Work.**

Technique_____

Technique_____

Technique_____

Technique_____

Technique_____

Technique_____

Exercise 3.2 (continued)   **Basic All-Purpose Powder Development. Mount Your Work.**

Technique_____

Technique_____

Technique_____

Technique_____

Technique_____

Technique_____

Exercise 3.2 (continued)   **Basic All-Purpose Powder Development. Mount Your Work.**

Technique_____

Technique_____

Technique_____

Technique_____

Technique_____

Technique_____

Exercise 3.2 (continued)   **Basic All-Purpose Powder Development. Mount Your Work.**

Technique_____

Technique_____

Technique_____

Technique_____

Technique_____

Technique_____

Exercise 3.2 (continued)   **Basic All-Purpose Powder Development. Mount Your Work.**

Technique_____

Technique_____

Technique_____

Technique_____

Technique_____

Technique_____

Practical Exercise 3.3: Latent Impression Development with Magnetic Powder

The purpose of this section is to identify, develop, and lift latent impressions using magnetic powders. In this practical exercise, you will compare black and white magnetic powders applied with your magnetic wand. After you have developed the prints, you will lift the print using rubber lifters, hinge lifters, and lifting tape. Much the same as all-purpose powders, magnetic powder works well on nonporous surfaces. The added benefit is that magnetic powder can also be used on porous surfaces with some success. One word of caution is that magnetic powder is fingerprint powder suspended in metal shavings which are then brushed onto the impression. Excess powder is removed when the metal shavings are removed with the magnet which is the wand. If you attempt to reuse the powder, you will use powder that has a greater metal concentration and a lower concentration of fingerprint powder. This can adversely affect the quality of your developed impression. Because of this phenomenon, you should not reuse the powder when you move from crime scene to crime scene. You will see that there are times when use of magnetic powder is preferable. Some investigators find that they are able to use magnetic powder only on horizontal surfaces, others find that they are also able to use magnetic powder on vertical surfaces. Remember, the person working next to you may find a different combination that works for him/her.

At the conclusion of the practical exercise, you will prepare a written report that will identify your steps taken and your results and will compare the various methods. Finally, in your report, determine which method you prefer and why. You have been given an ample number of pages to mount your impressions for future reference.

Equipment Needed

1. Adequate porous and nonporous smooth surface materials to develop impressions (for example, red-colored plastic plates, Styrofoam cups, bottles, cans, and paper plates)
2. Black magnetic powder
3. White magnetic powder
4. Magnetic wand
5. Clear-back hinge lifters
6. White-back hinge lifters
7. Black-back hinge lifters
8. White-back rubber lifters
9. Black-back rubber lifters
10. Lifting tape, 2 in. wide

Complete the Exercises

Exercise 3.3.1: Black Magnetic Powder

In this portion of the exercise, you will use black magnetic powder to develop impressions. Black powder works well on light-colored surfaces.

1. Examine a nonporous surface for impressions. Ensure the surface will allow a good contrast for black powder. Remember that the use of oblique lighting techniques will likely aid in your search.
2. Prepare a shallow dish out of a piece of paper by folding up the sides to put the powder in.
3. Place a small amount of black magnetic powder in the paper dish. This makes loading your wand much easier.
4. Dip your wand into the powder until you have a good amount of magnetic powder adhering to it. You will end up with a small ball of powder adhering to the magnetic wand.
5. Using a painting motion, lightly run the powder over the area of the impression. Care must be taken not to destroy the print with the wand. Touch the print with the powder, not the wand.
6. When the impression begins to develop and ridge detail is evident, place the wand over your powder dish and pull the plunger up, which will drop the magnetic filings back into your dish.
7. Hold the wand slightly above the impression and use the magnetic properties to remove excess powder. You should end up with a nice clean impression.

Exercise 3.3.1.1: White-Back or Clear Hinge Lifters

1. Open your hinge lifter and apply the lifter from the open end toward the hinge portion of the lift. Carefully rub out the air pockets as you press down.
2. Lift the hinge lifter and carefully close.
3. Mark the lift in accordance with department policy.

Exercise 3.3.1.2: White-Back Rubber Lifter

1. Repeat the above steps but lift the impression with a white-back rubber lifter. The lifting technique is the same.

Exercise 3.3.1.3: Clear Lifting Tape

When you are ready to lift, follow these steps:

1. If you are on a horizontal surface, pull an ample amount of tape off the roll so that you can hold each end above the impression.
2. Hold the tape in a "U" shape and allow the center of the tape to touch the impression. Then gently press down, while at the same time working out any air bubbles.

3. If you are on a vertical surface, use gravity to your advantage and let the weight of the tape roll assist you in eliminating bubbles. In this case, you would apply the tape above the impression and work your way down the tape until the impression is completely covered.

4. Cut the tape and adhere it to a clean clear piece of acetate (such as a clear document protector).

5. Mark the lift in accordance with your departmental policy.

Exercise 3.3.2: White Magnetic Powder.

In this portion of the exercise you will use white magnetic powder instead of black. The use of white powder would be indicated on very dark surfaces where black powders would not provide the contrast required to observe ridge detail.

All of your actions in this section are the same as they were for the black powder. The only difference is you will use white powder in lieu of black. Remember that you will need to create a new dish for your white powder.

Exercise 3.3.2.1: Clear or Black-Back Hinge Lifters

1. Repeat the above steps but lift the impression with a clear or black-backed hinge lifter as described previously.

Exercise 3.3.2.2: Black-Back Rubber Lifters

1. Repeat the above steps but lift the impression with a black-back rubber lifter as described previously.

Exercise 3.3.2.3: Clear Lifting Tape

1. Repeat the above steps but lift the impression with a roll of clear lifting tape as described previously.

Document Your Activity

To complete this exercise, you need to document your findings. Include factors such as ease of use, time involved, quality of the print, or if the print is reversed. Did you find that you liked white powder better than black? How did cleanup compare to the amount of cleanup needed for all-purpose powder? In this report you should also compare and contrast the use of magnetic vs. traditional powders.

NOTES

Exercise 3.3   Magnetic Powder Development. Mount Your Work.

Technique_____

Technique_____

Technique_____

Technique_____

Technique_____

Technique_____

Exercise 3.3 (continued) **Magnetic Powder Development. Mount Your Work.**

Technique_____

Technique_____

Technique_____

Technique_____

Technique_____

Technique_____

Practical Exercise 3.4: Latent Impression Development with Superglue and All-Purpose and Magnetic Powders

The purpose of this section is to identify, document, and develop latent impressions on surfaces using a chemical process commonly referred to as "superglue." In this practical exercise, you will learn how to develop latent impressions using cyanoacrylate ester, more commonly referred to as superglue. You will use four different variations of development. These methods will include ambient air and three different accelerants.

At the conclusion of the practical exercise, you will prepare a written report that will identify your steps taken and your results and will discuss reasons and occasions when you would use this fingerprint development technique.

Equipment Needed

1. Adequate porous and nonporous surfaces (for example, plastic plates, glasses, writing paper, and a soda can)
2. Cyanoacrylate ester (superglue) in a liquid form
3. Cyanoacrylate ester (superglue) in commercially available, resealable superglue pads
4. Superglue fuming chamber (24-qt plastic container with snap-on lid)
5. Superglue accelerator materials consisting of:
   - Coffee cup warmer
   - Cotton balls which have been soaked in a baking soda bath and allowed to dry (one per item to develop)
   - Cotton balls which have been soaked in a household bleach bath and allowed to dry (one per item to develop)
   - Aluminum foil
   - Clean water, 12 oz
   - Styrofoam drinking cup, 8 oz
6. Black magnetic powder
7. Magnetic powder wand
8. Hinge lifters
9. Rubber lifters
10. Lifting tape
11. Masking tape

Complete the Exercises

Preparation

Prior to initiating the examination, you must identify a suitable nearly airtight container for the development of the impressions. A multitude of containers are available. For this experiment we will use a large clear plastic storage container with a snap-on lid. This container must have a hole in it large enough to accommodate an electric plug.

Ensure that you are in an area of adequate ventilation. You should conduct this exercise outside if the ambient air temperature is at least 60°F. If you are indoors, you should be either under an exhaust hood or in an area with doors and windows that can be opened. This is needed as some individuals find the fumes from superglue fuming to be overbearing.

You will also make use of a test print to assist you in determining if development is complete.

Exercise 3.4.1: Use of Ambient Air

1. Prior to any other actions, cover the hole in the container with masking tape.

2. Place one porous and one nonporous object in the plastic container, standing each on end if possible. A nonporous test print will let you know when development of all the objects in the tank is complete.

3. Place a test print on a different nonporous object and place this in the container where it will be readily visible from the outside during development.

4. Place a small amount (3 or 4 oz) of water in a cup in a container to enhance the humidity.

5. Place several drops of superglue onto a piece of aluminum foil that you fashion into a foil "cup" (totaling about the size of a dime) and place in the bottom of the container. Alternately, open one of the premade superglue packets and place it on the bottom of the container.

6. Close the container and set it aside. Check the items (by looking through the side) every 15 minutes until good ridge detail is observed on your test print object.

7. After good detail is observed, open the container and ventilate to the outside, thereby removing the fumes. Document development time.

8. Use all-purpose or magnetic fingerprint powder to develop the print and lift it using your favorite fingerprint lifting medium. If you need guidance concerning development of the impression with powder, refer to your prior exercises.

As an optional exercise, repeat the above activity but this time, tape a premade superglue packet to the top of the chamber with masking tape. This will demonstrate that the cyanoacrylate ester fumes are heavier than air and will settle to the lower portions of the chamber, onto your evidence.

Exercise 3.4.2: Use of Heat as an Accelerant

Prior to any other actions, remove the tape from the hole in the container, place the coffee cup warmer in the container, and tape the hole over with the plug protruding from the box. Plug the coffee cup warmer into a working electrical outlet and leave the warmer in the OFF position.

1. Place a porous and a nonporous object in the tank, standing each on end if possible.

2. Place a nonporous object with a test print on it in the container. A nonporous test print will let you know when development of all the objects in the tank is complete.

3. Place 3 or 4 oz of water in a cup in the container to enhance the humidity.

4. Place several drops of superglue into a foil "cup" (totaling about the size of a dime) and place on top of the coffee cup warmer.

5. Turn the warmer to the ON position, seal the container, and set aside.

6. Check the items (by looking through the side) every 5 minutes until good ridge detail is observed on your test print object.

7. After good detail is observed, open the container and ventilate outside, thereby removing the fumes. Document development time.

8. Use all-purpose or magnetic fingerprint powder to develop the print and lift it using your favorite fingerprint lifting medium.

Exercise 3.4.3: Use of Baking Soda as an Accelerant

1. Place a porous and a nonporous object in the tank (which has now had the coffee cup warmer removed and the hole covered), standing each on end if possible.

2. Place a nonporous object with a test print on it in the container. A nonporous test print will let you know when development of all the objects in the tank is complete.

3. Place 3 or 4 oz of water in a cup in a container to enhance the humidity.

4. Place a small amount of aluminum foil in the tank and place a cotton ball that has been previously saturated with the baking soda bath on the foil.

5. Place several drops of superglue on the cotton ball (about the same amount as you used in heat acceleration). Use of the superglue on the pre-saturated cotton ball will produce fumes more quickly.

6. Seal the container and set it to the side. Check the items (by looking through the side) every 5 minutes until good ridge detail is observed on your test print object.

7. After good detail is observed, open the container and ventilate outside removing the fumes. Document development time.

8. Use all-purpose or magnetic fingerprint powder to develop the impression and lift it using your favorite fingerprint lifting medium.

Exercise 3.4.4: Use of Bleach as an Accelerant

1. Place a porous and a nonporous object in the tank, standing on end if possible.

2. Place a nonporous object with a test print on it in the container. A nonporous test print will let you know when development of all the objects in the tank is complete.

3. Place 3 or 4 oz of water in a cup in the container to enhance the humidity.

4. Place a small amount of aluminum foil in the tank and place a cotton ball that has been previously saturated with bleach on the foil.

5. Place several drops of superglue on the cotton ball (about the same amount as you used in heat acceleration). Use of the superglue on the pre-saturated cotton ball will produce fumes more quickly.

6. Seal the container and set it to the side. Check the items (by looking through the side) every 5 minutes until good ridge detail is observed on your test print object.

7. After good detail is observed, open the container and ventilate outside to remove the fumes. Document development time.

8. Use all-purpose or magnetic fingerprint powder to develop the impression and lift it using your favorite fingerprint lifting medium.

Document Your Activity

To complete this activity, you need to document your findings. Include in your report any observations you have about the pros and cons of each method. Include ease of use, time involved, cleanup, and cost in your report. Did you determine any difference in the quality of the impression based upon whether it was porous or nonporous? Did the use of an accelerant benefit you in any way? If so, which accelerant and how did it benefit you? Finally, do you see any benefit to using superglue processing techniques?

NOTES

Exercise 3.4   Superglue Development. Mount Your Work.

Technique_____

Technique_____

Technique_____

Technique_____

Technique_____

Technique_____

Exercise 3.4 (continued)   **Superglue Development. Mount Your Work.**

Technique_____

Technique_____

Technique_____

Technique_____

Technique_____

Technique_____

Practical Exercise 3.5: Latent Impression Development on Textured Surfaces

The purpose of this section is to identify, develop, and lift latent impressions on textured surfaces using a variety of products. In this practical exercise, you will accomplish two tasks. First, you will compare all-purpose and magnetic powders with regard to latent impression development on textured surfaces. Second, you will compare various media used to lift the latent impressions that have been developed. You will compare lifting with commercially available gel glue, Liqui-lift™ lifting material, Mikrosil silicone material, and Diff-lift tape.

At the conclusion of the practical exercise, you will prepare a written report that will identify the steps taken and your results and will compare the various methods. Finally, in your report, identify which method you prefer and why.

Equipment Needed

1. Five nonporous textured-surface materials to develop impressions (plastic children's footballs work well)
2. Black all-purpose powder
3. White all-purpose powder
4. Black magnetic powder
5. White magnetic powder
6. Two camel's hair brushes
7. Two fiberglass brushes
8. Two magnetic powder wands
9. Clear-back hinge lifters
10. White-back hinge lifters
11. White-back rubber lifters
12. Lifting tape, 2 in. wide
13. Liqui-lift brand lifting material
14. Commercially available gel glue
15. Clean drinking straw
16. Diff-lift brand (or equivalent) lifting tape
17. Mikrosil brand (or equivalent) silicone material
18. Clean glass plate for mixing silicone lifting material
19. Wooden stick for stirring (tongue depressor)

Complete the Exercises

The first portion of this exercise is to develop the latent impressions using techniques learned in the all-purpose powder and magnetic powder exercises. You will develop the impressions first with all-purpose powder and then with magnetic powder. After you have developed the impressions, you will practice lifting techniques with various media.

Exercise 3.5.1: Development

In this section you will compare all-purpose powder and magnetic powder to develop impressions. In each exercise in this part you will develop four separate impressions with each method.

1. Prepare black all-purpose powder and your preferred brush.
2. Examine the surface for impressions. Ensure the surface will allow a good contrast for black powder. Use oblique lighting techniques to assist you in locating a latent impression.
3. Follow the guidelines set out in the all-purpose powder development exercise to develop four separate latent impressions with black all-purpose powder and your preferred brush.
4. Prepare white all-purpose powder and your preferred brush.
5. Examine the surface for impressions. Ensure the surface will allow a good contrast for white powder. Use oblique lighting techniques to assist you in locating a latent impression.
6. Follow the guidelines set out in the all-purpose powder development exercise to develop four separate latent impressions with white all-purpose powder and your preferred brush.
7. Prepare black magnetic powder and magnetic wand.
8. Examine the surface for impressions. Ensure the surface will allow a good contrast for black powder. Use oblique lighting techniques to assist you in locating a latent impression.
9. Follow the guidelines set out in the magnetic powder development exercise to develop four separate latent impressions with black magnetic powder and your magnetic wand.
10. Prepare white magnetic powder and magnetic wand.
11. Examine the surface for impressions. Ensure the surface will allow a good contrast for white powder. Use oblique lighting techniques to assist you in locating a latent impression.
12. Follow the guidelines set out in the magnetic powder development exercise to develop four separate latent impressions with white magnetic powder and your magnetic wand.

Exercise 3.5.2: Lifting Techniques

You should now have sixteen different latent impressions in front of you, four from each of the above methods. In this section of our exercise, you will examine four separate lifting methods. You will attempt to lift one of each type of impression with each of the development methods. These lifts will be the basis of your comparison in your written report.

Gel Glue

1. For this exercise, you need to use commercially available gel glue. Lift one impression from each development method above.

2. On one side of the impression, squeeze out an amount of gel glue equal to the size of the impression. Pour the glue in a line adjacent to one edge of the impression.

3. With a regular drinking straw, blow at an oblique angle, across the glue and toward the impression. This will cause the glue to migrate over the impression. Continue to blow with a constant gentle amount of pressure until the impression is completely covered.

4. Allow the impression to completely dry before you attempt to lift it.

Liqui-lift

1. For this exercise you need to use commercially available Liqui-lift (or equivalent) textured-surface impression material. (Liqui-lift is a gluelike substance that dries quick and neater than traditional gel glue.) Process one impression from each development method above.

2. On one side of the impression, squeeze out an adequate amount of the glue that it would cover the impression.

3. With a regular drinking straw, blow at an oblique angle, across the glue until it completely covers the impression.

4. Allow the impression to completely dry before you attempt to lift it.

Mikrosil

1. For this exercise, use either commercially available Mikrosil brand silicone lifting material, or another commercially available silicone lifting material. (Note that this is the same material that will be used in tool mark collection.) Process one impression from each development method above.

2. To prepare the impression material, place your glass plate on a stable horizontal surface and squeeze out a line of the silicone material. The silicone material is in the larger of the two tubes in the kit.

3. Next, squeeze out an equal length line of the hardener. The hardener is the smaller of the two tubes. The lines should be of equal length however the hardener line will be of significantly less volume.

4. Thoroughly mix the two lines of material together with the wood tongue depressor.

5. Using the tongue depressor, paint the impression material over the impressions you developed, until completely covered.

6. Allow the impression to completely dry before you attempt to lift it.

Diff-lift

1. For this exercise, use commercially available Diff-lift, which is essentially a thick fingerprint tape capable of being pushed into the texture of most surfaces. Lift one impression from each development method above.
2. Apply the Diff-lift tape from the roll as though you were applying regular fingerprint lifting tape.
3. With a blunt object (such as the eraser of a pencil) push the tape down until it visually covers the entire impression.
4. Lift the tape as you would a normal impression.

After you have developed and processed all of the various impressions, allow them all to dry completely. Document your drying time. You will likely need the corner of a sharp object to get some of the impressions lifted. Turn the dried impression over and observe the impression. Use clear tape to mount the impressions on the following pages.

Document Your Activity

To complete this exercise, you need to document your findings. You should include factors such as ease of use, time involved, drying time, quality of the print, if the print is reversed, and cleanup required. Finally, take a position as to your favorite combinations of powder, brush, and lifting material and defend your position. Which did you prefer and why?

NOTES

Exercise 3.5   Textured Surface Development. Mount Your Work.

Technique_____

Technique_____

Technique_____

Technique_____

Exercise 3.5 (continued)   **Textured Surface Development. Mount Your Work.**

Technique_____

Technique_____

Technique_____

Technique_____

133

Exercise 3.5 (continued)   **Textured Surface Development. Mount Your Work.**

Technique_____

Technique_____

Technique_____

Technique_____

Exercise 3.5 (continued)   **Textured Surface Development. Mount Your Work.**

Technique_____

Technique_____

Technique_____

Technique_____

Practical Exercise 3.6: Small Particle Reagent Development

The purpose of this section is to identify and document the development of latent impressions on surfaces not conducive to other powder or chemical development methods. To accomplish this, a product has been developed that is a combination of molybdenedisulfide powder in a detergent solution. This has a number of commercial names; however, the generic name that this process is most widely known as is "small particle reagent." Most commonly small particle reagent is thought of as being used on wet surfaces. Although wet surface development is clearly the most popular application, small particle reagent also works very well on galvanized metals such as fence posts and electric transformer casings.

At the conclusion of the practical exercise, you will prepare a written report that will identify the steps taken and your results and will discuss reasons and occasions when you would use this fingerprint development technique. On the pages immediately after your report, space has been provided to mount your lifts.

Equipment Needed

1. Adequate nonporous articles (such as a plastic plate) that have latent impressions on them and have gotten wet
2. White and black color small particle reagent, parts one (reagent) and two (clean water)
3. Running water
4. A small plastic cup or large plastic syringe such as a turkey baster
5. Two glass baking pans (9 × 12 in size)
6. Hinge lifters
7. Rubber lifters
8. Lifting tape

Complete the Exercises

Just as with all of your other latent impression exercises, the color choice is mandated by both conditions and preference. You will use both black and white small particle reagents in this exercise to assist you in your decision.

Exercise 3.6.1: Portable Objects

White Small Particle Reagent

1. Place the object you wish to develop for latent impressions into a glass baking pan.
2. Hold the object at an angle and bathe the area you suspect to have an impression with small particle reagent by gently pouring the liquid over the object until an impression is observed.

3. Move the object being printed to a second glass baking pan tub and bathe the object using clear water from a slow running tap or from a small beaker until the impression is clear. The plastic syringe works well to accomplish this. Alternatively, you can use a spray bottle with clean water and mist the area until all excess reagent is removed. The small particle reagent will wick away from the surface quickly.

4. Once the majority of the reagent and water has wicked away leaving the area dry, lift the impression, using one of the three traditional lifting media (black-back hinge lifters, black-back rubber lifters, or clear lifting tape).

Black Small Particle Reagent

1. Repeat the above steps but use black small particle reagent and white-backed lifters to accomplish the exercise.

Exercise 3.6.2: Nonportable Objects

White Small Particle Reagent

1. When you have identified a nonmoveable object with a potential latent impression, gently mist the area with small particle reagent until an impression is apparent. This impression may not be perfectly clear, yet you will still likely see ridge detail.

2. Use a second bottle, which contains clean water, and gently mist away the excess small particle reagent.

3. When the impression area has developed and you are satisfied with the ridge detail, and the majority of the excess water has wicked away leaving the area dry, lift the impression using one of the three traditional media (black-back hinge lifters, black-back rubber lifters, or clear lifting tape).

Black Small Particle Reagent

1. Repeat the above steps but use black small particle reagent and white-backed lifters to accomplish the exercise.

Document Your Activity

To complete this exercise, you will need to document your findings. Prepare a report that characterizes the ease of use of this material. Discuss the times when you would use this development method and your observations concerning ease of use. Be sure to cover difficulty, cleanup, cost, and quality of the impression. Which did you prefer and why?

NOTES

_____
_____
_____
_____
_____
_____
_____
_____
_____
_____
_____
_____
_____
_____
_____
_____
_____
_____
_____
_____
_____
_____
_____
_____
_____
_____
_____
_____

Exercise 3.6   Small Particle Reagent Development. Mount Your Work.

Technique_____

Technique_____

Technique_____

Technique_____

Casts and Impressions

In this section you will be introduced to another aspect of evidence collection, the ability to use impression material to develop and collect both two- and three-dimensional impressions. This will not only include footwear evidence, but will also introduce you to lifting tool mark impressions with silicone material.

Impression evidence identification and collection is one of the most destructive examinations that can be employed. When you apply impression material onto a two- or three-dimensional item of potential evidence, you will forever alter the appearance of that evidence. If you do not properly document the item prior to attempting to cast it, you risk destroying the item without obtaining any useable evidence. Not only is the evidentiary value of the item in jeopardy if not properly documented, but the admissibility of that item may also be called into question. Courts have routinely ruled that evidence must be available for review by both sides in a trial, and a lack of documentation may place that review in peril. For these reasons, a photographic documentation element has been included in each of these exercises. Note that there are no specific photography directions included; however, a photography log has been included and proper photography techniques should be employed. Finally, several pages have been included to mount your photographs for future reference.

Exercise 4.1 Casts

```
        S R Z E I C Y U
        O Z N H M K R S
        F P         J G
        D Y         U O
O G A B C I T S A L P E L B A L A E S E R L
W A Y L C X N K P H P U L D G L Z G L H A Y
C L J T P B H E O V C I E A Z V G W T N T Q
U A A K G Z O T R G Q N P J A N Y V O X C R
B U P I T H O C V U T U Z W I P U I U N C B
W B Q Z Z G S H E A D C Y T V J S W G L E A
L Q R Z R I X L L U D Y F H E N Q H D R G G
B A L A N O I S N E M I D E E R H T M C J M
P N P F A G T R W D S U B M E R G E D G D R
F H G I H O M A G N E T I C P O W D E R Y E
T S C T N F K I S J S D N W P K P N T V G U
Q I I E Z Y R L T W O T O O N E U L Y H V H
S N O W P R I N T W A X Z F L X I M T Q G N
G T E L L S Z Z T N I R P E S A E R G P X S
```

1. The material used by most crime investigators to make a case
2. A two-dimensional impression, in a mechanics garage, for example
3. The preferred fingerprint powder used to develop two-dimensional impressions
4. The technique used to photograph an impression; enhanced ridge detail
5. One of the tasks to be accomplished prior to making a cast, involves a camera
6. The container in which to mix the impression material
7. The process of gently placing impression material into a wet impression
8. One of the tasks to be accomplished prior to making a cast; involves a pencil and paper
9. A commercial product used to firm up fragile impressions prior to making a cast
10. Classification of an impression that is underwater
11. An impression with depth, such as in sand
12. An impression that has no depth
13. The ratio of dental stone to water

Photographic Log

Case Number_____Date/Time Begun_____

Detective Assigned Case_____

Photographer_____

Camera System _____Serial Number_____

Film Type_____ISO_____ # of Exposures on Roll _____

Lens(es) Used (Type/Serial Number) _____

Flash Information: Type/Serial Number:_____

Explanation of abbreviations: Camera position was eye level unless otherwise indicated.
DA = Directly above (perpendicular to subject of photograph)
N = Normal lens; M = Macro lens; W = Wide angle lens

Exposure #	Time	F/Stop	Shutter Speed	Distance	Description

Page _____ of _____ pages

Crime Scene Processing Laboratory Manual and Workbook

Case Number_____ (Photographic Log Continued)

Exposure #	Time	F/Stop	Shutter Speed	Distance	Description

Practical Exercise 4.2: Basic Three-Dimensional Casting

The purpose of this section is to identify and lift three-dimensional impressions in soft soil using casting material known as "dental stone." You will prepare a mixture of dental stone and determine the best technique (for you) to pour a cast. At the conclusion of the practical exercise, you will prepare a written report that will identify the steps taken and your results and will include anything that might assist you in the future with lifts.

Equipment Needed

1. Dental stone (at least 24 oz per impression)
2. Mixing container
3. Framing material (commercially available plastic or metal frames work well)
4. Water (at least 12 oz per impression)
5. Wooden spatula
6. Resealable plastic bags (one per impression)
7. Camera, either digital or film, with adequate film or disk space to document the exercise
8. Hairspray (either aerosol or pump)
9. Measuring device
10. Paper and pencil
11. Soft soil three-dimensional impressions

Complete the Exercise

As with any practical exercise, preparation will determine success or failure. When it comes to casting, this is even more critical as the mixture of impression material, while generally accurate, is an inexact recipe. You may need more or less water for the amount of impression material you use.

1. Locate (or create) a three-dimensional impression in soft soil. Because of the academic nature of this exercise, locate an impression with good ridge detail. Keep in mind that at an actual crime scene, you would process any impression, no matter how much ridge detail you thought you could see.
2. After you have located the impression you wish to cast, determine the lowest point in the impression.
3. Photograph the impression to document the condition it was in when initially observed.
4. Remove any loose debris (do not remove any imbedded debris).
5. Rephotograph the impression to document the removal of loose debris.
6. Place your frame on all sides of the impression.

7. Before attempting to pour the cast, you must solidify the impression. This is accomplished with hair spray. Hold the hairspray container about 18 in. above the impression and spray the hairspray over the impression parallel to the ground, allowing the hairspray to cascade onto the impression. This will strengthen the impression and minimize the destruction of ridges from the casting material. Note that this step may not always be needed, such as in dried mud; however, it is a good protective measure for soft soil impressions.

8. Place your casting material (dental stone) into the resealable plastic bag.

9. Slowly add water while gently mixing the casting material. As a comparison, this action is similar to kneading bread. You may prefer to use a wooden spatula or mixing stick, until the majority of the material is mixed together, then seal the bag and use your hands to remove any lumps.

10. Mix your dental stone and water until you get the consistency of thin pancake batter. You may need to add either additional water or dental stone powder mix until you attain the consistency that you desire.

11. Allow the mixture to set for about 2 min. This will allow the chemicals to interact with each other and the mixture will set up slightly. Care must be taken not to wait too long.

12. Position yourself outside the impression in a manner so that you can observe the flow of the casting material across the impression.

13. Cut a small hole in one bottom corner of the bag. This will act as a spigot to pour your impression material into the impression.

14. Pour the mixture into the impression, using a gloved hand or stiff piece of cardboard to break the fall of the material.

15. Pour the mixture into the lowest point on the impression and allow the mixture to flow on its own over the entire impression. Although you could speed the process by moving across the impression, damage to the fragile ridge detail in the impression is more likely if you do so.

16. Allow the mixture to harden to the touch and apply a subsequent layer(s) for strength. Ideally, the final product will be about 1-in. thick.

17. As the final coat begins to harden, etch the cast with a north directional indicator and appropriate identification markings, in accordance with departmental policy for evidence identification.

18. Allow your cast to harden for a minimum of 1 hour, and then pick up the entire cast, including the border. If the frame comes off at this time, it will not damage the cast, however if it remains adhered to the cast, allow it to remain.

19. After the cast has been allowed to cure for 24 hours, you will be able to remove the frame.

    (Note that if this were actual evidence, you would package up the cast without any further action and submit it for examination to your crime laboratory.)

20. *Because this is an academic environment*, gently brush off any excess dirt with a soft paint brush. You may wish to use a very light water flow to further rinse off the cast. This will enable observation in class.

21. Photograph your final product.

Document Your Activity

To complete this exercise, you will need to document your findings. Include factors such as drying time, cleanup, quality of the cast, and ways you could improve the cast. How easy or difficult did you find this exercise? Did you find utility in pouring a cast, and do you think you would use it at a crime scene?

An extra place for a spare photograph is available should you choose to take an additional photograph.

NOTES

Exercise 4.2   Basic Casting. Mount Your Work.

NOTES_____

NOTES_____

NOTES_____

NOTES_____

Practical Exercise 4.3: Three-Dimensional Submerged Impression Casting

The purpose of this section is to identify and lift three-dimensional impressions that are submerged in water using dental stone. Much as you cannot control the environment in which a crime is committed in, neither can you control the place that a criminal steps. It is very common to find an impression in a puddle or on a shoreline near a large body of water. You may even find yourself presented with an impression that is in a body of flowing water such as a stream. Although we would certainly like to only process pristine crime scenes, these all too common findings must also be properly processed. In this practical exercise, you will attempt three different methods of applying dental stone to submerged impressions to determine the best technique (for you) to pour a cast. As you will no doubt discover when completing this exercise, you will see ways that you can modify the steps to best fit your capabilities.

At the conclusion of the practical exercise, you will prepare a written report that will identify your steps taken and your results and will include anything that might assist you in the future with lifts.

Equipment Needed

1. Dental stone (at least 24 oz per impression)
2. Mixing container
3. Framing material
4. Damming material (such as a bucket with the bottom cut out)
5. Water (at least 12 oz per impression)
6. Flour sifter
7. Wooden spatula
8. Large plastic syringe such as a turkey baster
9. Resealable plastic bags (one per impression)
10. Camera, either digital or film, with adequate film or disk space to document the exercise
11. Hairspray
12. Measuring device
13. Paper and pencil
14. Soft soil three-dimensional submerged impressions

Complete the Exercises

As with any practical exercise, preparation will determine success or failure. When it comes to casting, this is even more critical as the mixture of impression material, while generally accurate, is an inexact recipe. You may need more or less water for the amount of impression material you use.

Exercise 4.3.1: Dam and Drain Method

In this method, you will attempt to remove as much of the water from the impression as possible. The premise of this method is that using a damming device that you place around the impression, you will suction off the majority of the water, leaving only a small amount of liquid which can be absorbed into the cast.

1. Locate (or create) a three-dimensional impression that is completely submerged in stagnant water, such as a mud puddle. Because of the academic nature of this exercise, locate an impression with good ridge detail. Keep in mind that at an actual crime scene, you would process any impression, no matter how much ridge detail you thought you could see.

2. Photograph the impression to document the original condition when discovered. Remember that when you insert the scale, it must be on the same plane as the actual impression, so you may have to dig out an area immediately adjacent to the impression to lower the height of the scale. Specific directions can be found in the photography exercises in this workbook.

3. Place a dam around the impression. Depending upon the depth of the water, you may also be able to use a regular casting frame.

4. Using the suction device, suction out as much water as possible, leaving the impression with only a small amount of water.

5. Using your flour sifter, fill the sifter with dry dental stone and gently sift the powder over the impression. The dental stone will cover the entire impression and begin to mix with the remainder of the moisture in the impression and result in the beginnings of the cast.

6. Allow that mixture to set up for 3 or 4 minutes while you prepare a mixture of liquid dental stone to create the cast.

7. Prepare a traditional cast as detailed in previous exercises. Note that this will be slightly different as the cast that you have been creating will absorb the liquid and cracks may begin to appear, these cracks are abated by merely allowing the mixture to fill in the cracks. Ensure that your mixture is sufficiently thin which will allow the mixture to flow freely into the cracks.

8. Care must be taken to not apply too much mixture at one time. It is better to have multiple thin layers than one thick layer.

9. Allow the mixture to harden to the touch and apply a subsequent layer(s) for strength. Ideally, the final product will be about 1-in. thick.

10. As the final coat begins to harden, etch the cast with a north directional indicator and appropriate identification markings, in accordance with departmental policy for evidence identification.

11. Allow your cast to harden for a minimum of 1 hour, and then pick up the entire cast, including the border. If the frame comes off at this time, it will not damage the cast; however, if it remains adhered to the cast, allow it to remain.

12. After the cast has been allowed to cure for 24 hours, you will be able to remove the frame.

    (Note that if this were actual evidence, you would package up the cast without any further action, and submit it for examination to your crime laboratory.)

13. *Because this is an academic environment*, gently brush off any excess dirt with a soft paint brush. You may wish to use a very light water flow to further rinse off the cast. This will enable observation in class.

14. Photograph your final product.

Exercise 4.3.2: Dam and Sift Method

The key difference between this method and the dam and drain method is that in this method, you will use the water that is present in the impression and gently sift the dental stone material into the water until the impression is completely covered.

1. Locate (or create) a three-dimensional impression that is completely submerged in stagnant water such as a mud puddle. Because of the academic nature of this exercise, locate an impression with good ridge detail. Keep in mind that at an actual crime scene, you would process any impression, no matter how much ridge detail you thought you could see.

2. Photograph the impression to document the original condition when discovered.

3. Place a dam around the impression. Depending upon the depth of the water, you may also be able to use a regular casting frame.

4. Fill the flour sifter with dental stone powder and sift the dental stone into the water in the dammed impression. As you begin, sift in only a small amount and allow it to float to the bottom of the liquid and onto the impression.

5. Sift in the dental stone, in "coats," allowing the dental stone to absorb the water and sink to the bottom of the impression.

6. When you have sifted enough dental stone into the impression so that the impression is devoid of water, allow it to begin to dry.

7. Prepare a traditional cast as detailed in previous exercises. Note that this will be slightly different because the cast that you have been creating will absorb the liquid and cracks may begin to appear, these cracks are abated by merely allowing the mixture to fill in the cracks.

8. Care must be taken to not apply too much mixture at one time. It is better to have multiple thin layers than one thick layer.

9. Allow the mixture to harden to the touch and apply a subsequent layer(s) for strength. Ideally, the final product will be about 1-in. thick.

10. As the final coat begins to harden, etch the cast with a north directional indicator and appropriate identification markings, in accordance with departmental policy for evidence identification.

11. Allow your cast to harden for a minimum of 1 hour, and then pick up the entire cast, including the border. If the frame comes off at this time, it will not damage the cast; however, if it remains adhered to the cast, allow it to remain.

12. After the cast has been allowed to cure for 24 hours, you will be able to remove the frame.

    (Note that if this were actual evidence, you would package up the cast without any further action, and submit it for examination to your crime laboratory.)

13. *Because this is an academic environment*, gently brush off any excess dirt with a soft paint brush. You may wish to use a very light water flow to further rinse off the cast. This will enable observation in class.

14. Photograph your final product.

Exercise 4.3.3: Dam, Drain, Dry, and Pour Method

This is the most problematic of the three methods introduced here for making a cast of a submerged impression. This method would likely be employed only when you have an impression that is in a claylike material that when dry will hold the original shape without much alteration.

1. Locate (or create) a three-dimensional impression that is completely submerged in stagnant water such as a mud puddle. Because of the academic nature of this exercise, locate an impression with good ridge detail. Keep in mind that at an actual crime scene, you would process any impression, no matter how much ridge detail you thought you could see.
2. Photograph the impression to document the original condition when discovered.
3. Place a dam around the impression. Depending upon the depth of the water, you may also be able to use a regular casting frame.
4. Using the suction device, suction out as much water as possible, leaving the impression with a minor amount of water.
5. Allow the impression to completely dry and then prepare a traditional cast as detailed in previous exercises. This could take several hours.
6. Care must be taken not to pour too much mixture down at one time. It is better to have multiple thin layers than one thick layer.

   (Note that if this were actual evidence, you would package up the cast without any further action, and submit it for examination to your crime laboratory.)
7. *Because this is an academic environment,* gently brush off any excess dirt with a soft paint brush. You may wish to use a very light water flow to further rinse off the cast. This will enable observation in class.
8. Photograph your final product.

Document Your Activity

To complete this activity, you must prepare a report to document your actions. Include an analysis of the different methods discussed and your success with each. Which method worked best for you? Why do you believe that you were most successful with that method? Can you think of a way to modify these methods to make them work better for your environment? What about the quality of your casts? How important is photography in the casting process?

NOTES

Exercise 4.3   Three-Dimensional Casting. Mount Your Work.

Exercise 4.3 (continued)   Three-Dimensional Casting. Mount Your Work.

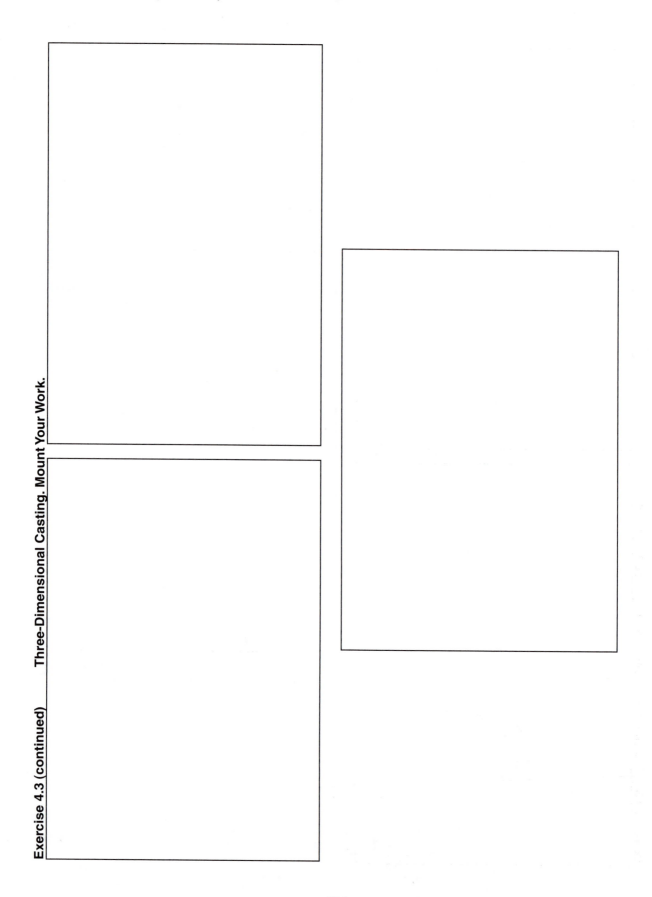

Exercise 4.3 (continued)   **Three-Dimensional Casting. Mount Your Work.**

Practical Exercise 4.4: Casting a Two-Dimensional Impression

The purpose of this section is to identify and lift two-dimensional impressions that are discovered at a crime scene using dental stone. In this practical exercise, you will identify various types of two-dimensional impressions, develop those impressions using different fingerprint powders, and then cast the impressions with dental stone. Part of the exercise is to determine which powder(s) work best for you to develop the impressions.

At the conclusion of the practical exercise, you will mount photographs as a permanent record of your work, and then prepare a written report which will identify your steps taken and your results and will include anything that might assist you in the future with this type of evidence.

Equipment Needed

1. Black all-purpose powder
2. White all-purpose powder
3. Black magnetic powder
4. White magnetic powder
5. Camel's hair brush
6. Fiberglass brush
7. Magnetic powder wand
8. Dental stone (at least 24 oz per impression)
9. Mixing container
10. Framing material (cardboard cut to size works well)
11. Scissors
12. Low tack tape
13. Water (at least 12 oz per impression)
14. Wooden spatula
15. Resealable plastic bags (1 per impression)
16. Tongue depressor (1 per impression)
17. One can of nonstick cooking spray
18. Camera, either digital or film, with adequate film or disk space to document the exercise
19. Measuring device
20. Paper and pencil

Complete the Exercises

Exercise 4.4.1: Patent Grease Impressions (Sealed Surface)

Casting a patent grease impression is no different from a traditional cast, with only minor modifications. Steps are as follows:

1. Locate or create a patent two-dimensional impression. (If you need to create one for this exercise, fingerprint ink on a shoe sole works well.) Keep in mind that at an actual crime scene, you would process any impression, no matter how much ridge detail you thought you could see.

2. Photograph the impression prior to casting, both with and without scale.

3. Prepare a frame around the two-dimensional impression. To prepare the frame, use cardboard (such as file folder material) cut into strips about 3-in. wide, held together with tape. Once the frame is prepared, use low tack "painters tape" and tape the frame to the floor. As you complete the frame, place a tongue depressor under one part of the frame and into the area that will be cast, yet outside the actual impression, so that it protrudes out of the frame. Completely encircle the frame with tape. The tongue depressor must protrude from the frame so that you can loosen the completed cast. Omitting this step may result in a severe suction situation that could preclude your getting up the cast.

4. Make a cast as you would for a three-dimensional soft surface impression.

5. Pour dental stone into the frame from one spot, allowing the mixture to flow across the entire impression.

6. Pour successive coats until you have a cast that is about 1-in. thick. Ensure that you mark your cast in accordance with your departmental policy.

7. Allow your cast to harden for a minimum of 1 hour, and then pick up the entire cast, including the border. If the frame comes off at this time, it will not damage the cast; however, if it remains adhered to the cast, allow it to remain.

8. After the cast has been allowed to cure for 24 hours, you will be able to remove the frame.

9. Photograph your final product.

Exercise 4.4.2: Patent Wet Impressions (Sealed Surface)

A wet patent impression, such as a boot impression on concrete, will fade and presents unique challenges. This fugitive evidence is frequently overlooked unless it is expeditiously processed. You must keep this factor in mind when you assess your crime scene. These impressions will dry quickly, and once dry, chances of lifting an impression are not as good. You will attempt to develop these impressions using both all-purpose powder and magnetic powder. The purpose of the powder is to enhance the impression. It is likely that you will develop a technique that you will prefer to use when you develop impressions such as these.

Exercise 4.4.2.1: Black All-Purpose Powder

1. Locate or create a patent two-dimensional impression. (If you need to create one for this exercise, step on a wet towel and then walk across a sealed concrete or tile floor. Ensure that

159

enough water is on the bottom of the shoe to create a patent impression. Keep in mind that at an actual crime scene, you would process any impression, no matter how much ridge detail you thought you could see.

2. Photograph the impression.

3. Develop the impression using black all-purpose fingerprint powder and your preferred brush (either fiberglass or camel's hair brush) just as you would any other latent impression. EXTREME CARE MUST BE TAKEN NOT TO USE TOO MUCH POWDER!

4. Photograph the developed impression.

5. Prepare a frame around the two-dimensional impression. The preparation of this frame is identical to the directions above. Ensure that you include the tongue depressor.

6. Make a cast following the above directions.

7. Allow your cast to harden for a minimum of 1 hour, and then pick up the entire cast, including the border. If the frame comes off at this time, it will not damage the cast; however, if it remains adhered to the cast, allow it to remain.

8. After the cast has been allowed to cure for 24 hours, you will be able to remove the frame.

9. Photograph your final product.

Exercise 4.4.2.2: Black Magnetic Powder

1. Locate or create a patent two-dimensional impression. (If you need to create one for this exercise, you may do so in the same manner as described above.)

2. Photograph the impression.

3. Develop the impression using black magnetic fingerprint powder and a magnetic powder wand as you have previously learned. EXTREME CARE MUST BE TAKEN NOT TO USE TOO MUCH POWDER!

4. Photograph the developed impression.

5. Prepare a frame around the two-dimensional impression. The preparation of this frame is identical to the directions above. Ensure that you include the tongue depressor.

6. Make a cast following the directions above.

7. Allow your cast to harden for a minimum of 1 hour, and then pick up the entire cast, including the border. If the frame comes off at this time, it will not damage the cast; however, if it remains adhered to the cast, allow it to remain.

8. After the cast has been allowed to cure for 24 hours, you will be able to remove the frame.

9. Photograph your final product.

Exercise 4.4.3: Latent Dry Impressions (Sealed Surface)

Exercise 4.4.3.1: Black All-Purpose Powder

1. Using oblique lighting techniques, locate a latent impression.

2. Develop the latent impression using black all-purpose powder and your preferred brush. USE CAUTION NOT TO APPLY EXCESSIVE POWDER!

3. Photograph the developed impression.

4. Prepare a frame around the impression as detailed above. Ensure that you include the tongue depressor.

5. Make a cast following the above directions.

6. Allow your cast to harden for a minimum of 1 hour, and then pry up the entire cast, including the border. If the frame comes off at this time, it will not damage the cast; however, if it remains adhered to the cast, allow it to remain.

7. After the cast has been allowed to cure for 24 hours, you will be able to remove the frame.

8. Photograph your final product.

Exercise 4.4.3.2: Black Magnetic Powder

1. Using oblique lighting techniques, locate a latent impression.

2. Develop the latent impression using black magnetic powder and your preferred brush. USE CAUTION NOT TO APPLY EXCESSIVE POWDER!

3. Photograph the developed impression.

4. Prepare a frame around the impression as detailed above. Ensure that you include the tongue depressor.

5. Make a cast following the above directions.

6. Allow your cast to harden for a minimum of 1 hour, and then pry up the entire cast, including the border. If the frame comes off at this time, it will not damage the cast; however, if it remains adhered to the cast, allow it to remain.

7. After the cast has been allowed to cure for 24 hours, you will be able to remove the frame.

8. Photograph your final product.

Exercise 4.4.4: Wet Patent Impressions (Unsealed Surfaces)

Unsealed surfaces will absorb liquid and cause the liquid to wick into the surface, which obliterates ridge detail in the image very quickly. Because of this phenomenon, a sense of urgency must be instilled in the crime scene investigator when faced with these impressions. The technique for development and lifting is similar to those used on sealed surfaces; however, an additional step must be employed.

Exercise 4.4.4.1: Black All-Purpose Powder

1. Locate or create a patent two-dimensional impression. (If you need to create one for this exercise, you may do so in the same manner as described above.)

2. Photograph the impression.

3. Develop the impression using black all-purpose powder and your preferred brush. EXTREME CARE MUST BE TAKEN NOT TO USE TOO MUCH POWDER!

4. Photograph the developed impression.

5. Prepare a frame around the two-dimensional impression. The preparation of this frame is identical to the directions above. Ensure that you include the tongue depressor.

6. After the impression is developed and the frame is formed, the additional step of spraying the impression with an aerosol nonstick cooking spray, to ease lifting of the impression, should be accomplished. Spray the area above the impression from a height of about 24 in., allowing the mist to cascade onto the impression.

7. Make a cast following the above directions.

8. Allow your cast to harden for a minimum of 1 hour, and then pry up the entire cast, including the border. If the frame comes off at this time, it will not damage the cast; however, if it remains adhered to the cast, allow it to remain.

9. After the cast has been allowed to cure for 24 hours, you will be able to remove the frame.

10. Photograph your final product.

Part 4.4.4.2: Black Magnetic Powder

1. Locate or create a patent two-dimensional impression. (If you need to create one for this exercise, you may do so in the same manner as described above.)

2. Photograph the impression.

3. Develop the impression using black magnetic fingerprint powder and a magnetic powder wand. EXTREME CARE MUST BE TAKEN NOT TO USE TOO MUCH POWDER!

4. Photograph the developed impression.

5. Prepare a frame around the two-dimensional impression. The preparation of this frame is identical to the directions above. Ensure that you include the tongue depressor.

6. After the impression is developed and the frame is formed, the additional step of spraying the impression with an aerosol nonstick cooking spray, to ease lifting of the impression, should be accomplished. Spray the area above the impression from a height of about 24 in., allowing the mist to cascade onto the impression.

7. Make a cast following the above directions.

8. Allow your cast to harden for a minimum of 1 hour, and then pry up the entire cast, including the border. If the frame comes off at this time, it will not damage the cast; however, if it remains adhered to the cast, allow it to remain.

9. After the cast has been allowed to cure for 24 hours, you will be able to remove the frame.

10. Photograph your final product.

Document Your Activity

To complete this exercise, you will need to document your findings. Include factors such as how effective the barrier you created was, drying time, cleanup, quality of the cast, and ways you could improve the cast. You should also discuss any challenges associated with magnetic versus regular powder, sealed versus unsealed surfaces. Which method did you prefer? When would you use this method of lifting an impression?

NOTES

Exercise 4.4   Two-Dimensional Casting. Mount Your Work.

Exercise 4.4 (continued)   **Two-Dimensional Casting. Mount Your Work.**

Exercise 4.4 (continued)   Two-Dimensional Casting. Mount Your Work.

Exercise 4.4 (continued)   Two-Dimensional Casting. Mount Your Work.

Exercise 4.4 (continued)   Two-Dimensional Casting. Mount Your Work.

Exercise 4.4 (continued)   Two-Dimensional Casting. Mount Your Work.

Exercise 4.4 (continued)   Two-Dimensional Casting. Mount Your Work.

Practical Exercise 4.5: Tool Mark Impression

The purpose of this section is to identify, document, develop, and lift impressions in relatively soft surfaces such as a doorframe. You will use silicone impression material to accomplish this. There are several commercially available products. One example is a product named Mikrosil™; however, any similar product will work.

At the conclusion of the practical exercise, prepare a written report which will identify your steps taken, your results, and include anything that might assist you in the future with lifts.

Equipment Needed

1. Silicone casting material kit (generally two separate tubes: one, the actual silicone material and one, a hardener)
2. Flat surface such as a piece of glass
3. Tongue depressor
4. Camera, either digital or film, with adequate film or disk space to document the exercise
5. Paper and pencil
6. Three-dimensional tool marks

Complete the Exercise

As with any practical exercise, preparation will determine success or failure. When it comes to using silicone impression material, preparation is critical. Although you can use these materials at various temperatures, just like dental stone, you must allow adequate drying time. While it may take about 7 minutes to harden at room temperature, it will take significantly longer as the temperature rises. One of the biggest mistakes with the use of silicone lifting material is not allowing the material to set up properly. As you will also notice, this material can be used for latent fingerprints, shoe impressions, or any other impression that you want to collect. Additionally, you must remember that the use of silicone impression material is very invasive, and as such, proper photographic documentation cannot be overlooked.

Locate (or create) a three-dimensional tool mark in a piece of wood, a door frame, a window sill, or other similar surface. Because of the academic nature of this exercise, locate an impression with good visible ridge detail. Keep in mind that at an actual crime scene, you would process any impression, no matter how much ridge detail you thought you could see.

1. Photograph the tool mark to document the condition of the tool mark when discovered. Make sure you take one photograph without scale and one with scale.
2. Impression materials come in a variety of colors; however, for tool marks, a dark color, generally brown, is usually appropriate.

3. To prepare the impression material, place your glass plate on a stable horizontal surface and squeeze out a line of the silicone material. The silicone material is in the larger of the two tubes in the kit.

4. Next, squeeze an equal length line of the hardener out. The hardener is the smaller of the two tubes in the kit. The lines should be of equal length; however, the hardener line will be of significantly less volume.

5. Thoroughly mix the two lines of material together with the wood tongue depressor.

6. Using the tongue depressor, paint the impression material over the tool mark you developed until completely covered.

7. Allow the mixture to harden to the touch before you attempt to pull the cast away from the impression material.

8. Remove the silicone material which will now be a flexible substance.

9. Photograph your final product for reference. Make sure to take one photograph without scale and one with scale.

10. Process this cast as a piece of moveable evidence in accordance with your departmental policies.

Document Your Activity

To complete this exercise, you need to document your findings. Include factors such as drying time, cleanup, quality of the cast, and ways you could improve your technique. How easy or difficult did you find this exercise? Did you find utility in pouring a cast or do you think it would be easier to cut out the area that contains the impression? When might you contemplate cutting out part of a crime scene? Would you use this technique at a crime scene?

NOTES

Exercise 4.5   Tool Marks. Mount Your Work.

Part **5**

Bloodstain Evidence Documentation

In this section you will be introduced to bloodstain evidence. These exercises will not make you an expert in bloodstain evidence, nor will they equip you to reconstruct a crime scene from the bloodstain evidence present. Rather, they will enable you to draw some general conclusions about what events *may* have occurred. The exercises in this section consist of both paper-based and hands-on exercises. Bloodstain evidence identification and collection is extremely invasive and destructive. When you collect a bloodstain, you completely obliterate the stain. Swabbing a bloodstain for collection will forever alter the appearance of that stain. As such, it is important that you properly photograph all bloodstain evidence. For this reason, a photographic documentation element has been included in each of these exercises. You have been provided with ample space to mount your photographs. Let this section not only enhance your knowledge of bloodstains, but further your photographic abilities.

Exercise 5.1 Bloodstain Terminology

```
                                        L R U B
                                        C E D V
                                        I P C Y
                                        E W
                                        T N
                         Y P S Z S U I O
                 O X W E J T Y I Q B R A A T I
         L K E Z R I R I E D A F X F C Y H R T D I T
         X H J A H D P E X C F U L W L N S S U Z V C
         P A E X P I R A T O R Y B L O O D E R Q E A
         N S A T E L L I T E S P A T T E R N A O P Y
         W I C R V N V S P P J Z T R Z Q R I T B A R
         J G O X V E A W O L F E V I S S A P I D T A
         P R M J F C O T A E Q A N E P I W S O W T L
         F F T L U X S Q Q S Q O R L L D Y K N K E L
         C L O R E T T A P S T C A P M I Y U S B R I
         F W R W A G H E P E F S C Z W O B F T J N P
         C Q N I K I I B T T H D B Q R V O D A X T A
         I Q N J M H L L N I H S W S N J R P I T R C
         R Q M Y B S E F Q G Z Y V Y P A A D N L A X
         Y Q U C T K G K M E O G I R           N X
         M H G G S T P                         S Q
                                               F F
                                               E E
                                               R Z
```

1. A blood flow caused by gravity and circulatory action

2. The force exhibited in the attraction of liquid to surfaces it is in contact with and its own surface tension

3. Stains created when blood is flung or projected from an object in motion

4. A gelatinous mass caused by the collection of blood cells

5. A pattern of blood caused when liquid blood falls into another liquid

6. Blood forced from the mouth or nose under pressure, resulting in spatter

7. Patterns caused by the deposition of blood by flies

8. A radiating pattern of many small stains, created by a blood source being broken up by force

9. A blood flow caused by gravity alone, with no circulatory action involved

10. A contact transfer of blood from one object to another in which a recognizable image is present in the pattern

11. A series of stains caused by an object wet with blood coming in contact with a secondary target

12. Small stains created when droplets detach from another droplet as it impacts a target

13. An irregular stain caused by contact with a significant blood source (i.e., pooled blood)

14. A disturbance of a bloodstain showing a short passage of time between deposition and disturbance

15. Linear characteristics evident in both single drop stains and volume stains

16. The stain pattern created when a volume of blood impacts a target with minimal force

17. Transfer of blood onto a target by a moving object that is bloodstained

18. A pattern of individual venous blood drops; demonstrates movement

19. An area within a generally continuous bloodstain pattern that lacks bloodstains

20. A stain created when an object moves through a preexisting bloodstain on another surface

Photographic Log

Case Number_____Date/Time Begun_____

Detective Assigned Case_____

Photographer_____

Camera System _____Serial Number_____

Film Type_____ISO_____ # of Exposures on Roll _____

Lens(es) Used (Type/Serial Number) _____

Flash Information: Type/Serial Number:_____

Explanation of abbreviations: Camera position was eye level unless otherwise indicated.
DA = Directly above (perpendicular to subject of photograph)
N = Normal lens; M = Macro lens; W = Wide angle lens

Exposure #	Time	F/Stop	Shutter Speed	Distance	Description

Page _____ of _____ pages

Case Number_____ (Photographic Log Continued)

Exposure #	Time	F/Stop	Shutter Speed	Distance	Description

Practical Exercise 5.2: Bloodstain Measurement

The purpose of this section is to familiarize you with the mechanics of measuring bloodstains, which have been provided for you.

Equipment Needed

1. Magnifying loop or digital calipers
2. Paper and pen
3. Flashlight

Complete the Exercise

Measuring the length and width of a bloodstain at a crime scene is one of the most challenging aspects of bloodstain pattern interpretation. On the following page there are six photographs of bloodstains. You must measure those bloodstains in an attempt to determine the length and the width. Do not worry about whether the stains are one to one (actual life) size. The relationship of length to width will remain the same regardless of the size of the stain. Use either a magnifying loop or a digital caliper to measure the stain. There may be a measuring device on the photograph; however, you should use your actual measuring device.

Document Your Activity

To complete this exercise, you will need to document your findings. Document your reasoning for where you cut off the satellite spatter, or how you determined where the main portion of the stain ended for purposes of your measurements. Which device did you use to measure the stain? How easy or difficult did you find this exercise?

BLOODSTAIN MEASUREMENT NOTES

Exercise 5.2 Bloodstain Measurement Photographs.

Record the Length and Width of the Stains

	First Stain	Second Stain	Third Stain	Fourth Stain	Fifth Stain	Sixth Stain
Length						
Width						

Practical Exercise 5.3: Bloodstain Height

The purpose of this section is to acquaint you with the appearance of a bloodstain at a crime scene when dropped from different heights and onto different surfaces. Based upon your results, you will be able to draw conclusions about what may have transpired when you find blood evidence at a crime scene. At the conclusion of the practical exercise, you will mount your bloodstan photgraphs in the area provided. You will also need to record the size of the stains. Finally, you will prepare a written report that will identify your steps taken, your results, and any information that may benefit you in the future when you encounter bloodstain evidence at a crime scene.

Please note that although this exercise is designed to be conducted with bovine (cow) blood, universal precautions should be taken to ensure safety of all individuals involved. This is a team exercise.

Equipment Needed

1. Eyedropper
2. Bovine (cow) blood
3. Personal protective equipment (mask, goggles, gloves, suit)
4. Stepladder
5. Tape measure
6. Masking tape
7. A marker
8. Bloodstain measuring loop
9. Digital caliper
10. A camera, either digital or film
11. Piece of picture frame glass, (8 × 10 in. size)
12. Poster board (at least 12 × 12 in. size),
13. Carpet strips (at least 12 × 12 in. size)
14. Scrap wood (at least 12 × 12 in. size)
15. Floor tile (12 × 12 in. size)
16. Paper and pen
17. Ruler

Complete the Exercises

Exercise 5.3.1: General Preparation

1. Premeasure the various heights on the stepladder. For this exercise, you will use the heights of 4 in., 8 in., 24 in., 48 in., and 72 in.
2. Mark your ladder with a piece of masking tape at each height.
3. Have two members of the team don personal protective gear (at a minimum, goggles, mask, and gloves). One person will actually drop the blood, while the other will move the surfaces and align the dropper.
4. Have a third member of the team act as the photographer for the entire exercise. At the conclusion of the exercise, have the photographs developed (if film is used) or printed (if digital), and make copies for each team member.
5. You are now ready to drop blood onto the different surfaces.

Exercise 5.3.2: Glass

1. Load the eyedropper with the bovine blood.
2. With the assistance of a fellow student to align the dropper properly, hold the eyedropper 4 in. above the glass, and drop one or two drops of blood onto the glass. Annotate the height from which those drops were dropped.
3. Move to a clean area on the glass.
4. With the assistance of a fellow student to align the dropper properly, hold the eyedropper 8 in. above the glass, and drop one or two drops of blood onto the glass. Annotate the height from which those drops were dropped.
5. Move to a clean area on the glass.
6. With the assistance of a fellow student to align the dropper properly, hold the eyedropper 24 in. above the glass, and drop one or two drops of blood onto the glass. Annotate the height from which those drops were dropped.
7. Move to a clean area on the glass.
8. With the assistance of a fellow student to align the dropper properly, hold the eyedropper 48 in. above the glass, and drop one or two drops of blood onto the glass. Annotate the height from which those drops were dropped.
9. Move to a clean area on the glass.
10. With the assistance of a fellow student to align the dropper properly, hold the eyedropper 72 in. above the glass, and drop one or two drops of blood onto the glass. Annotate the height from which those drops were dropped.
11. Set the glass aside and allow the blood drops to dry.
12. When dry, photograph each stain with a scale in the photograph.

Exercise 5.3.3: Poster Board

1. Load your eyedropper with the bovine blood. With the assistance of a fellow student to align the dropper properly, hold the eyedropper 4 in. above the poster board, and drop one or two drops of blood onto the poster board. Annotate the height from which those drops were dropped.

2. Move to a clean area on the poster board.

3. With the assistance of a fellow student to align the dropper properly, hold the eyedropper 8 in. above the poster board, and drop one or two drops of blood onto the poster board. Annotate the height from which those drops were dropped.

4. Move to a clean area on the poster board.

5. With the assistance of a fellow student to align the dropper properly, hold the eyedropper 24 in. above the poster board, and drop one or two drops of blood onto the poster board. Annotate the height from which those drops were dropped.

6. Move to a clean area on the wood.

7. With the assistance of a fellow student to align the dropper properly, hold the eyedropper 48 in. above the poster board, and drop one or two drops of blood onto the poster board. Annotate the height from which those drops were dropped.

8. Move to a clean area on the poster board.

9. With the assistance of a fellow student to align the dropper properly, hold the eyedropper 72 in. above the poster board, and drop one or two drops of blood onto the poster board. Annotate the height from which those drops were dropped.

10. Set the poster board aside and allow the blood drops to dry.

11. When dry, photograph each stain with a scale in the photograph.

Exercise 5.3.4: Wood

1. Load your eyedropper with the bovine blood.

2. With the assistance of a fellow student to align the dropper properly, hold the eyedropper 4 in. above the wood, and drop one or two drops of blood onto the wood. Annotate the height from which those drops were dropped.

3. Move to a clean area on the wood.

4. With the assistance of a fellow student to align the dropper properly, hold the eyedropper 8 in. above the wood, and drop one or two drops of blood onto the wood. Annotate the height from which those drops were dropped.

5. Move to a clean area on the wood.

6. With the assistance of a fellow student to align the dropper properly, hold the eyedropper 24 in. above the wood, and drop one or two drops of blood onto the wood. Annotate the height from which those drops were dropped.

7. Move to a clean area on the wood.

8. With the assistance of a fellow student to align the dropper properly, hold the eyedropper 48 in. above the wood, and drop one or two drops of blood onto the wood. Annotate the height from which those drops were dropped.

9. Move to a clean area on the wood.

10. With the assistance of a fellow student to align the dropper properly, hold the eyedropper 72 in. above the wood, and drop one or two drops of blood onto the wood. Annotate the height from which those drops were dropped.

11. Allow the blood drops to dry.

12. When dry, photograph each stain with a scale in the photograph.

Exercise 5.3.5: Carpet

1. Load your eyedropper with the bovine blood.

2. With the assistance of a fellow student to align the dropper properly, hold the eyedropper 4 in. above the carpet, and drop one or two drops of blood onto the carpet. Annotate the height from which those drops were dropped.

3. Move to a clean area on the carpet.

4. With the assistance of a fellow student to align the dropper properly, hold the eyedropper 8 in. above the carpet, and drop one or two drops of blood onto the carpet. Annotate the height from which those drops were dropped.

5. Move to a clean area on the carpet.

6. With the assistance of a fellow student to align the dropper properly, hold the eyedropper 24 in. above the carpet, and drop one or two drops of blood onto the carpet. Annotate the height from which those drops were dropped.

7. Move to a clean area on the carpet.

8. With the assistance of a fellow student to align the dropper properly, hold the eyedropper 48 in. above the carpet, and drop one or two drops of blood onto the carpet. Annotate the height from which those drops were dropped.

9. Move to a clean area on the carpet.

10. With the assistance of a fellow student to align the dropper properly, hold the eyedropper 72 in. above the carpet, and drop one or two drops of blood onto the carpet. Annotate the height from which those drops were dropped.

11. Allow the blood drops to dry.

12. When dry, photograph each stain with a scale in the photograph.

Exercise 5.3.6: Floor Tile

1. Load your eyedropper with the bovine blood.

2. With the assistance of a fellow student to align the dropper properly, hold the eyedropper 4 in. above the floor tile, and drop one or two drops of blood onto the tile. Annotate the height from which those drops were dropped.

3. Move to a clean area on the floor tile.

4. With the assistance of a fellow student to align the dropper properly, hold the eyedropper 8 in. above the floor tile, and drop one or two drops of blood onto the tile. Annotate the height from which those drops were dropped.

5. Move to a clean area on the floor tile.

6. With the assistance of a fellow student to align the dropper properly, hold the eyedropper 24 in. above the floor tile, and drop one or two drops of blood onto the tile. Annotate the height from which those drops were dropped.

7. Move to a clean area on the floor tile.

8. With the assistance of a fellow student to align the dropper properly, hold the eyedropper 48 in. above the floor tile, and drop one or two drops of blood onto the tile. Annotate the height from which those drops were dropped.

9. Move to a clean area on the floor tile.

10. With the assistance of a fellow student to align the dropper properly, hold the eyedropper 72 in. above the floor tile, and drop one or two drops of blood onto the tile. Annotate the height from which those drops were dropped.

11. Allow the blood drops to dry.

12. When dry, photograph each stain with a scale in the photograph.

Document Your Activity

Use either a magnifying loop or an electronic caliper to measure the length and width of all of the stains. Record those measurements on the chart at the end of this exercise. In this exercise, it is not practical to attempt to mount the stains, as the stains have varied thicknesses. At the back of this exercise, several pages have been inserted for you to mount your photographs of the stains. As a reminder, ensure that you include a scale in your photographs. What do the stain sizes tell you? Is it possible to determine anything from this experiment? Be sure to include your observations about the relationship between height and surface.

NOTES

Exercise 5.3: Bloodstain Heights.
Record the Length and Width of Stains Dropped from Various Heights

		Glass	Poster Board	Wood	Carpet	Tile
4 in.	Length					
	Width					
8 in.	Length					
	Width					
24 in.	Length					
	Width					
48 in.	Length					
	Width					
72 in.	Length					
	Width					

Exercise 5.3   Bloodstain Height. Mount Your Work.

SURFACE_____ HEIGHT_____

SURFACE_____ HEIGHT_____

SURFACE_____ HEIGHT_____

SURFACE_____ HEIGHT_____

Exercise 5.3 (continued)   Bloodstain Height. Mount Your Work.

SURFACE_____ HEIGHT_____

SURFACE_____ HEIGHT_____

SURFACE_____ HEIGHT_____

SURFACE_____ HEIGHT_____

Exercise 5.3 (continued)   Bloodstain Height. Mount Your Work.

SURFACE_____ HEIGHT_____

SURFACE_____ HEIGHT_____

SURFACE_____ HEIGHT_____

SURFACE_____ HEIGHT_____

Exercise 5.3 (continued)   Bloodstain Height. Mount Your Work.

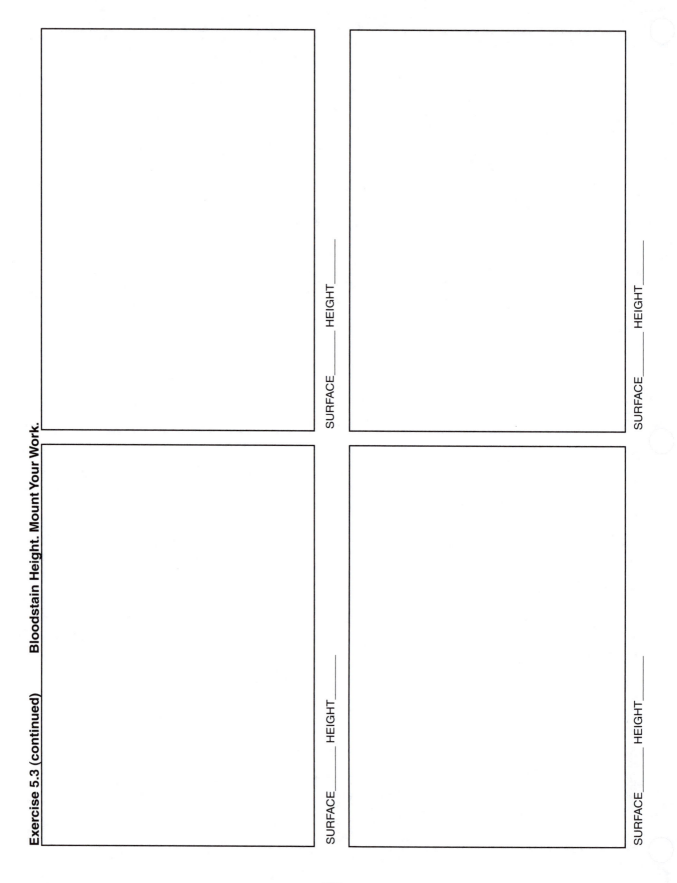

SURFACE_____ HEIGHT_____

SURFACE_____ HEIGHT_____

SURFACE_____ HEIGHT_____

SURFACE_____ HEIGHT_____

Exercise 5.3 (continued)   Bloodstain Height. Mount Your Work.

SURFACE_____ HEIGHT_____

SURFACE_____ HEIGHT_____

SURFACE_____ HEIGHT_____

SURFACE_____ HEIGHT_____

Exercise 5.3 (continued)   **Bloodstain Height. Mount Your Work.**

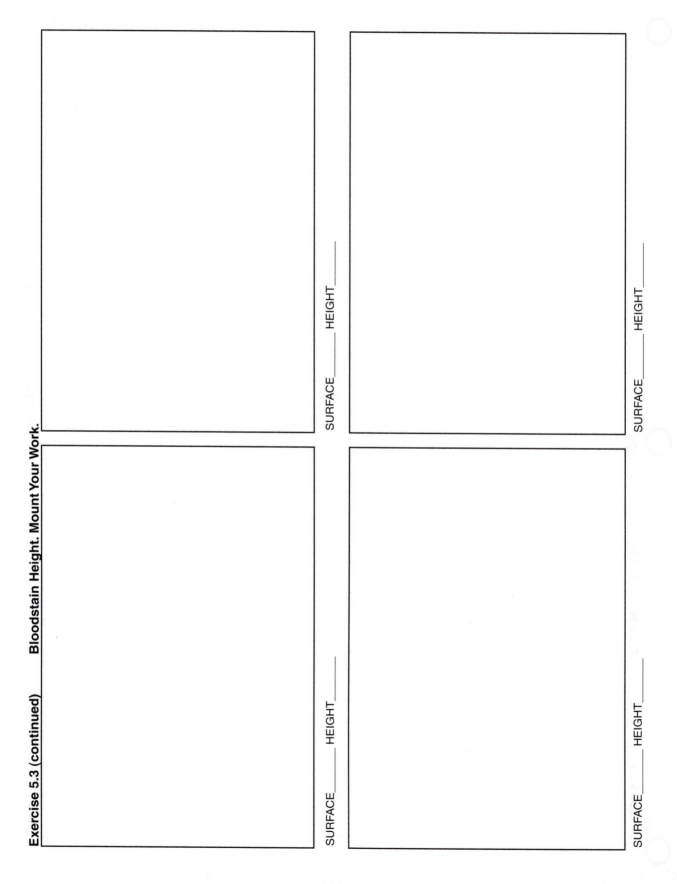

SURFACE_____ HEIGHT_____

SURFACE_____ HEIGHT_____

SURFACE_____ HEIGHT_____

SURFACE_____ HEIGHT_____

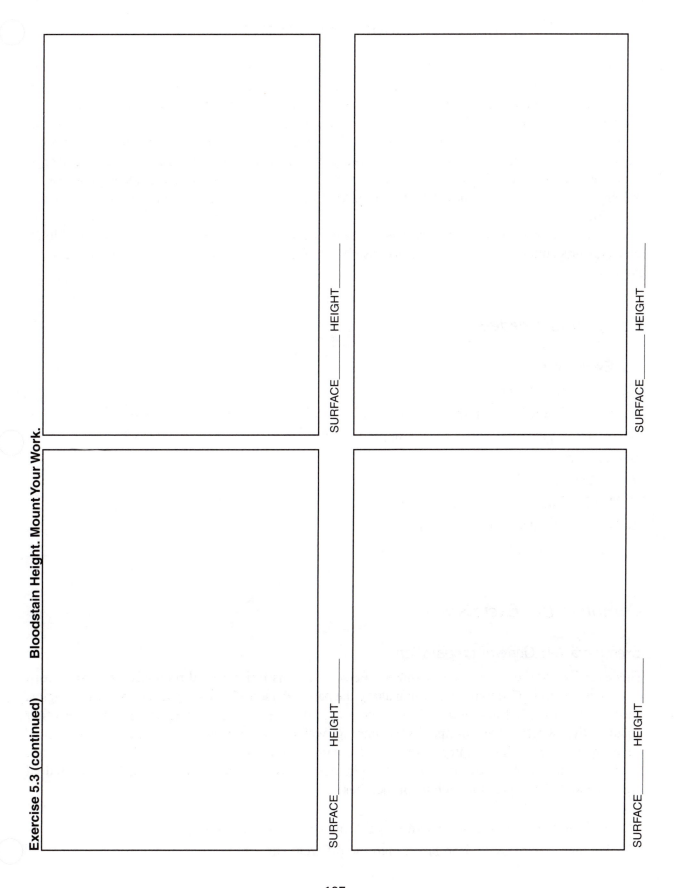

Exercise 5.3 (continued)   Bloodstain Height. Mount Your Work.

SURFACE_____ HEIGHT_____

SURFACE_____ HEIGHT_____

SURFACE_____ HEIGHT_____

SURFACE_____ HEIGHT_____

Practical Exercise 5.4: Bloodstain Motion

The purpose of this section is to familiarize you with the appearance of a bloodstain at a crime scene when dropped from a person walking, running, trotting, or staggering. In this practical exercise, you will drop blood from a height of about 3 ft onto rolled out paper. Based upon your results, you will be able to draw conclusions about what may have transpired when you find blood evidence at a crime scene. At the conclusion of the practical exercise, you will mount your bloodstain photographs or the bloodstains themselves in the area provided. You will also need to record the size of the stains. Finally, you will prepare a written report which will identify your steps taken, your results, and any information which may benefit you in the future when you encounter bloodstain evidence at a crime scene.

Please note that although this exercise is designed to be conducted with bovine (cow) blood, universal precautions should be taken to ensure safety of all individuals involved. This is a team exercise.

Equipment Needed

1. Eyedropper
2. Bovine (cow) blood
3. Personal protective equipment (mask, goggles, gloves, suit) for two members
4. A roll of paper, such as brown wrapping paper
5. Scissors
6. A marker
7. Digital caliper or magnifying loop
8. A camera, either digital or film
9. Paper and pencils

Complete the Exercises

Exercise 5.4.1: General Preparation

This exercise requires three team members. Person #1 dons full personal protective gear and drops blood while walking, trotting, or running along the paper. Person #2, wearing at a minimum, goggles, mask, and gloves, follows along behind person #1, circles the blood drops, and acts as a recorder documenting whether the 'dropper" was running, walking, or trotting, as well as the direction of the dropper's travel. Have a third member of the team act as the photographer for the entire exercise. At the conclusion of the exercise, have the photographs developed (if film is used) or printed (if digital) and make copies for each team member.

1. Roll out the wrapping paper in a straight line about 15 to 20 ft long.
2. You are now ready to drop blood onto the different surfaces.

Exercise 5.4.2: Walking

1. Load the eyedropper with bovine blood.
2. Walk along the paper with the eyedropper in your hand. As your hand swings naturally, gently squeeze the dropper causing blood drops to fall to the paper.
3. Circle the drops and annotate that they were from a "walk" and indicate the direction the person was walking.
4. Have your photographer photograph approximately five of the stains. Ensure you have a scale in the photograph.

Exercise 5.4.3: Trot or Jog

1. Load the eyedropper with bovine blood.
2. Trot or jog along the paper with the eyedropper in your hand. As your hand swings naturally, gently squeeze the dropper causing blood drops to fall to the paper.
3. Circle the drops and annotate that they were from a "jog" and indicate the direction the person was traveling.
4. Have your photographer photograph approximately five of the stains. Ensure you have a scale in the photograph.

Exercise 5.4.4: Run

1. Load the eyedropper with bovine blood.
2. Run along the paper with the eyedropper in your hand. As your hand swings naturally, gently squeeze the dropper causing blood drops to fall to the paper.
3. Circle the drops and annotate that they were from a "run" and indicate the direction the person was traveling.
4. Have your photographer photograph approximately five of the stains. Ensure you have a scale in the photograph.

Document Your Activity

1. Cut out five of the stains from each activity.

2. Use either a magnifying loop or an electronic caliper to measure the length and width of five stains from each exercise: walk, jog, and run. Record these measurements on the chart at the end of this exercise.

3. At the back of this exercise, several pages have been inserted for you to mount your photographs of the stains.

To complete this exercise, you will need to document your findings. What do the drops tell you? Is there any difference in what the drops look like depending upon the speed that you were traveling? Is there any difference in the distance between drops based upon your speed? Is it possible to determine anything from this experiment?

Exercise 5.4 Bloodstain Motion.
Measurement of Bloodstains Dropped While in Motion

		Walk	Jog	Run
First stain	Length			
	Width			
Second stain	Length			
	Width			
Third stain	Length			
	Width			
Fourth stain	Length			
	Width			
Fifth stain	Length			
	Width			

NOTES

Exercise 5.4   Bloodstain Motion. Mount Your Work.

SURFACE_____ HEIGHT_____

SURFACE_____ HEIGHT_____

SURFACE_____ HEIGHT_____

SURFACE_____ HEIGHT_____

Exercise 5.4 (continued) Bloodstain Motion. Mount Your Work.

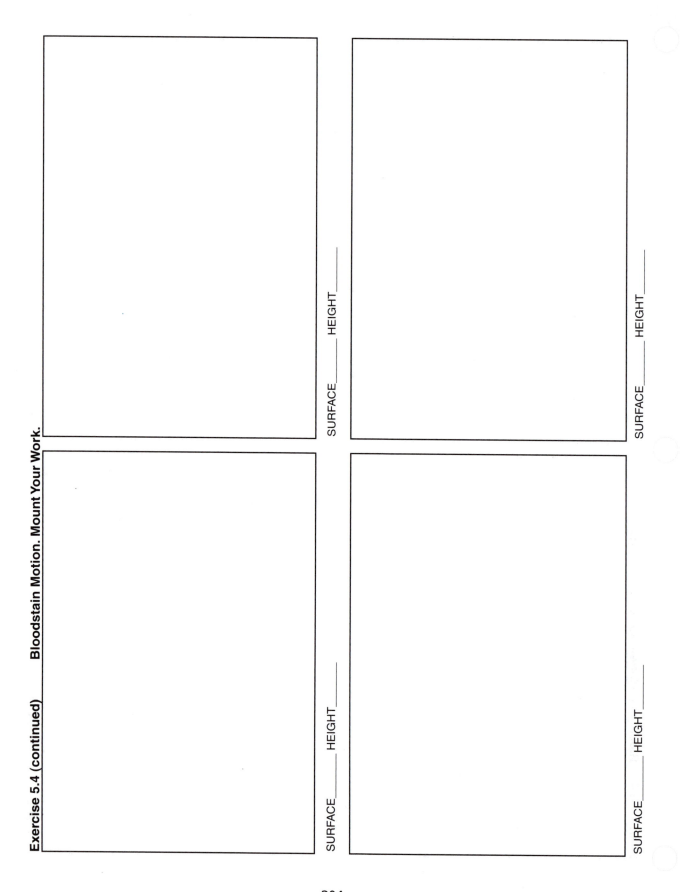

SURFACE_____ HEIGHT_____

SURFACE_____ HEIGHT_____

SURFACE_____ HEIGHT_____

SURFACE_____ HEIGHT_____

Exercise 5.4 (continued)   **Bloodstain Motion. Mount Your Work.**

SURFACE_____ HEIGHT_____

SURFACE_____ HEIGHT_____

SURFACE_____ HEIGHT_____

SURFACE_____ HEIGHT_____

Exercise 5.4 (continued)   Bloodstain Motion. Mount Your Work.

SURFACE_____ HEIGHT_____

SURFACE_____ HEIGHT_____

SURFACE_____ HEIGHT_____

SURFACE_____ HEIGHT_____

Practical Exercise 5.5: Bloodstain Angles

The purpose of this section is to familiarize you with the appearance of a bloodstain at a crime scene, which has been dropped from an angle. In this practical exercise, you will drop blood from a height of 24 in. onto pieces of poster board that are set to predetermined angles (from 10 to 90°) in an attempt to see what the droplet looks like after impact. For clarity, 10° is nearly vertical and 90° is horizontal. Based upon your results, you will be able to draw conclusions about what may have transpired when you find blood evidence at a crime scene. At the conclusion of the practical exercise, you will mount your bloodstain photographs or the bloodstains themselves in the area provided. You will also need to record the size of the stains. Finally, you will prepare a written report which will identify your steps taken, your results, and any information which may benefit you in the future when you encounter bloodstain evidence at a crime scene.

Please note that although this exercise is designed to be conducted with bovine (cow) blood, universal precautions should be taken to ensure safety of all individuals involved. This is a team exercise.

Equipment Needed

1. Personal protective equipment for two team members
2. Eyedropper
3. Bovine (cow) blood
4. Stepladder, straight-backed chair, or other item you can stabilize on at 24 in.
5. Tape measure
6. An adjustable compass, affixed to a clipboard (alternatively, a miter cut piece of wood) capable of making angles 10 to 90°
7. Camera, either digital or film, and adequate film or disk space
8. Magnifying loop or digital calipers
9. Ten pieces of poster board cut into 4 in. by 4 in. squares
10. Paper and pen

Complete the Exercises

Exercise 5.5.1: General Preparation

Have two members of the team don personal protective gear (at a minimum, goggles, mask, and gloves). One person will actually drop the blood while the other will change the angles and move the surfaces as well as align the dropper.

Have a third member of the team act as the photographer for the entire exercise. At the conclusion of the exercise, have the photographs developed (if film is used) or printed (if digital), and make copies for each team member. You are now ready to drop blood onto the different surfaces.

1. Set up your stepladder or straight-backed chair and measure 30 in. up. Make a tape mark. This height is needed as your target will be about 5 or 6 in. off the floor when you place the angle measuring device below the dropper and drop the blood.

2. Place your angle measuring device on the floor directly below the point from which you will drop the blood.

Exercise 5.5.2: Conduct the Exercise

1. Set the angle measuring device to the appropriate angle. Begin with 10° (nearly vertical).

2. Place a clean piece of poster board onto your measuring device at the appropriate angle. You will either hold the poster board in place with a clipboard or place it in the miter saw cut.

3. Have a second member of the team act as a holder and have the holder steady the clipboard or poster board (if in miter cut).

4. Drop two or three drops of blood onto the poster board from the height of 24 in. above the target. Care must be taken not to drop the drops on top of each other.

5. Lay the completed piece of poster board aside to dry.

6. Have your photographer photograph the stains. Ensure there is a scale in the photograph and that the camera is perpendicular to the poster board.

7. Repeat this angle until each member of the team has a card for blood dropped at 10°.

8. Repeat the above activity for each angle from 20 through 90° (20, 30, 40, 50, 60, 70, 80, and 90°).

Document Your Activity

Use either a magnifying loop or a digital caliper to measure the length and width of all of the stains. Record those measurements on the chart at the end of this exercise. At the back of this exercise, several pages have been inserted for you to mount your stains. As poster board has no real depth, it is possible to mount the actual stains if you so desire. Alternatively, you may wish to mount photographs. The amount of space required is the same.

After the droplets have dried, use the magnifying loop or digital caliper and measure the drops. Record your measurements on the chart. Include in your report the significance of the length of the tails on the stains or if you see satellite spatter. Finally, document your thoughts as to how this exercise may help you at future crime scenes.

Exercise 5.5 Bloodstain Angles Measurements.
Record the Length and Width of Stains Dropped from Known Angles

	First stain		Second stain	
	Length	Width	Length	Width
10°				
20°				
30°				
40°				
50°				
60°				
70°				
80°				
90°				

NOTES

Exercise 5.5   Bloodstain Angles. Mount Your Work.

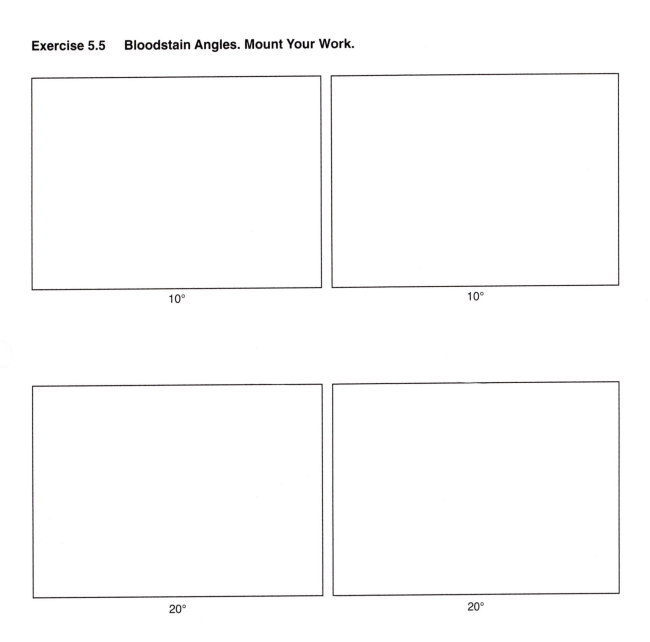

10°   10°

20°   20°

Exercise 5.5 (continued)   **Bloodstain Angles. Mount Your Work.**

30°

30°

40°

40°

Exercise 5.5 (continued)   **Bloodstain Angles. Mount Your Work.**

50°

50°

60°

60°

213

Exercise 5.5 (continued)   **Bloodstain Angles. Mount Your Work.**

70°

70°

80°

80°

Exercise 5.5 (continued)   **Bloodstain Angles. Mount Your Work.**

90°

90°

215